Short Bible Stories for Kids

A Collection of Essential Stories with
Discussion Points, Activities and
Questions for Ycung Readers

Cross & Crown Books

Table of Contents

Introduction

Welcome, Young Explorers!

You're about to embark on an amazing journey through some of the most fascinating stories ever told. These aren't just any stories – they're stories that have captivated people for thousands of years, been passed down through generations, and continue to inspire millions of people around the world today. As you turn these pages, you'll discover why these ancient tales still have so much to teach us in our modern world.

In this book, you'll meet incredible characters who faced challenges that might seem very different from yours at first glance. You'll discover how a shepherd boy named David defeated a giant against all odds, how a young queen named Esther found the courage to save her entire people, and how a man named Paul transformed from someone people feared into one of history's greatest teachers. You'll walk alongside Joseph as he goes from being sold into slavery to becoming one of the most powerful leaders in Egypt, and journey with Moses as he leads an entire nation to freedom.

But these aren't just stories about what happened long ago – they're stories about courage, wisdom, faith, and making tough choices, just like the ones you might face in your own life. When David faced Goliath, he was probably around your age, dealing with doubt and fear. When Esther had to speak up to the king, she had to overcome the same kind of nervousness you might feel when standing up for what's right.

What makes this book special is that we're going to do more than just read these stories. Together, we'll become time travelers and investigators, uncovering fascinating details about the past and discovering how these ancient stories connect to our lives today. As we explore each story, you'll:

- Uncover what daily life was really like in ancient times – from what people ate for breakfast to how they built their houses

- Explore amazing archaeological discoveries that help us understand these stories better

- Learn interesting facts about the places, cultures, and customs mentioned in each story

- Think about how these ancient stories connect to situations you might face at school, home, or with friends

- Discover the fascinating ways historians and archaeologists piece together information about the past

Throughout the book, you'll find special sections designed to make your journey even more exciting:

- "Time Travel Corner" will transport you back in time to experience the sights, sounds, and smells of the ancient world

- "Did You Know?" boxes are filled with fascinating facts that will surprise even your parents

- "Think About It" sections help you ponder the bigger questions and meanings behind each story

- "Your Turn" activities let you connect these stories to your own life in practical ways

- "Family Talk" sections provide great conversation starters for discussions with your family

- "Dig Deeper" segments share exciting archaeological discoveries that bring these stories to life

Whether you're reading this book on your own, sharing it with your family, or exploring it with friends, these stories will come alive in new and exciting ways. You might be surprised to find that people who lived thousands of years ago weren't so different from you – they had hopes and fears, dreams and doubts, just like we do today.

This book is designed to grow with you. You can read it straight through, or jump to stories that interest you most. You can read it quickly for the exciting plots, or slowly to absorb all the historical details. You might even find yourself coming back to these stories again and again, discovering new meanings each time you read them.

So, grab your metaphorical passport and archaeological tools – we're about to begin an adventure that will take us across thousands of years and thousands of miles, all while helping us understand ourselves, our world, and our faith better.

Turn the page, and let's begin our journey together!

Chapter 1:

In the Beginning - From Creation to the Great Flood

Have you ever looked up at the stars on a clear night and wondered how it all began? Or watched the waves crash on a beach and thought about who made them? For thousands of years, people have asked these same questions. The very first story in the Bible gives us some answers, and it starts with four powerful words: "In the beginning, God..."

Imagine absolute darkness and emptiness. No stars. No planets. No light at all. There was nothing but void and formless space. Then suddenly, with just a few words, everything changed. "Let there be light," God said, and brilliant light burst into existence, pushing back the darkness. This wasn't sunlight - the sun hadn't been created yet - but it was the first light ever to exist. God separated this light from the darkness, creating the very first day and night. This was Day One of our universe, but it was just the beginning of an amazing process of creation.

On the second day, God's voice rang out again across the emptiness. He created the sky, separating the waters above from the waters below. Imagine a vast dome of blue stretching overhead, with clouds forming and moving across this new expanse. The atmosphere that we breathe today, the clouds that bring us rain, and the blue sky we see every morning – all of these came into being on this day.

The third day brought even more dramatic changes. God gathered the waters below into one place, and dry land appeared. Mountains thrust up from beneath the waters, valleys carved their paths, and plains stretched out across the newly formed earth. But God wasn't finished yet. He spoke again, and the bare earth burst into life. Plants of every kind began to grow – tiny flowers pushed through the soil, grass spread across the plains, and trees reached their branches toward the sky. Each plant was created with seeds to reproduce, ensuring that life would continue and spread across the earth.

The fourth day brought the greatest light show the universe had ever seen. God created the sun to rule the day and the moon to rule the night. Stars appeared across the vast expanse of space – billions upon billions of them, from tiny twinkling points to massive burning giants. These lights weren't just for show; they were carefully placed to mark seasons, days, and years, creating the rhythms of time that we still follow today.

On the fifth day, God turned His attention to filling the seas and sky with living creatures. The waters suddenly teemed with life – from tiny fish to enormous whales, from darting schools of colorful tropical fish to creatures of the deep. Above, the sky came alive with birds of every kind. Eagles soared on thermal winds, tiny hummingbirds darted through the air, and songbirds filled the world with music for the first time.

The sixth day began with the creation of land animals. Imagine the excitement as animals of every kind came into being – powerful lions, gentle deer, industrious ants, and massive elephants. Each was unique, each had its purpose, and each was declared good by God. But the day wasn't over yet. God had saved His most special creation for last.

With particular care and purpose, God created humans – male and female – in His own image. Unlike the animals, humans were given unique abilities and responsibilities. They could think deeply, create beautiful things, make moral choices, and most importantly, have a relationship with God Himself. God blessed them and gave them an important job: to take care of the earth and all its creatures. They were to be stewards of creation, managing and protecting all that God had made.

Adam and Eve, the first humans, lived in a beautiful garden called Eden. It was a perfect place, where they could walk and talk with God freely. They had everything they needed, and their work of tending the garden was joyful and fulfilling. God gave them just one rule: they could eat from any tree in the garden except one – the tree of the knowledge of good and evil.

For a time, everything was perfect. The seventh day arrived, and God rested from His work of creation, setting an example for humans to follow. The world was exactly as He intended it to be – full of beauty, purpose, and harmony. Adam and Eve enjoyed their daily walks with God, their work in the garden, and their relationship with each other. They knew nothing of pain, shame, or hardship.

But this perfect world wouldn't stay perfect forever. One day, a clever serpent approached Eve in the garden. This wasn't just any snake – it was Satan in disguise, and he had a plan to ruin God's perfect creation. He found Eve near the forbidden tree and asked her a seemingly innocent question: "Did God really say you couldn't eat from any tree in the garden?"

Eve explained that they could eat from any tree except the one in the middle of the garden – the tree of the knowledge of good and evil. God had warned that if they ate from it, they would die. But the serpent twisted God's words, telling Eve, "You won't die. God just knows that when you eat it, you'll become like Him, knowing good and evil."

Eve looked at the fruit differently now. It did look delicious, and the promise of special knowledge was tempting. Making a decision that would change history forever, she took the fruit and ate it. She gave some to Adam, who was with her, and he ate it too.

Immediately, everything changed. Their eyes were opened, but not in the way they had hoped. For the first time, they felt shame and fear. They realized they were naked and quickly made clothes from fig leaves. When they heard God walking in the garden that evening, instead of running to meet Him as they usually did, they hid among the trees.

"Where are you?" God called, though He already knew the answer. When Adam and Eve finally came out of hiding, they had to admit what they'd done. But instead of taking responsibility, they started blaming others. Adam blamed Eve, and Eve blamed the serpent.

God's heart was broken, but He had to respond to their disobedience. He pronounced consequences for everyone involved. The serpent was cursed to crawl on its belly. Eve would have pain in childbirth and struggle in her relationship with Adam. Adam would have to work hard to grow food from ground that would now produce thorns and thistles. And hardest of all, Adam and Eve had to leave their perfect garden home. They would eventually die, just as God had warned.

As generations passed, things got worse. Adam and Eve's children and grandchildren spread across the earth, but they kept making bad choices. Cain, their first son, even killed his brother Abel out of jealousy. Violence and wickedness increased until the Bible tells us that "every inclination of the thoughts of the human heart was only evil all the time." This grieved God deeply – He regretted making humans and decided He would have to start over.

But there was one man who was different. Noah found favor with God because he was righteous and blameless among the people of his time. God shared His plans with Noah: He would send a great flood to cleanse the earth, but He would save Noah and his family. God gave Noah specific instructions to build a massive boat – an ark – that would keep them and two of every kind of animal safe during the flood.

Noah must have seemed crazy to his neighbors as he spent decades building a huge boat on dry land. They had never even seen rain before – the earth had only been watered by springs and mists! But Noah kept building, following God's instructions exactly. The ark was enormous: 450 feet long, 75 feet wide, and 45 feet high, with three decks and rooms for all the animals. Noah also warned people about the coming judgment, but no one outside his family believed him.

Finally, after many years of building, the ark was complete. God told Noah it was time. Noah's family – his wife, his three sons (Shem, Ham, and Japheth), and their wives – went into the ark. Animals began arriving in pairs, male and female of every kind. There were seven pairs of clean animals (those suitable for sacrifice and food) and one pair of all the others. For seven days, they filed into the ark while Noah's neighbors probably laughed and pointed. Then God himself shut the door.

What happened next was unlike anything the world had ever seen. The Bible says "all the springs of the great deep burst forth, and the floodgates of the heavens were opened." Rain fell for forty days and forty nights without stopping. Water erupted from underground springs and covered even the highest mountains. Everything outside the ark – every person, every animal, every bird – was swept away. The water covered the earth for 150 days.

But inside the ark, Noah and his family were safe, along with all the animals. Think about what life must have been like on the ark: feeding all those animals, cleaning their cages, dealing with the constant rocking of the boat on the waters. Noah and his family had to trust God completely during this time – they couldn't see where they were going or know how long they would be there.

Finally, God sent a wind to dry the earth. The waters slowly began to recede. After about five months, the ark came to rest on the mountains of Ararat. Noah sent out a raven to look for dry land, but it kept flying back and forth, finding nowhere to land. Then he sent out a dove, but it returned because the water still covered everything. Seven days later, he sent the dove out again. This time, it returned with a fresh olive leaf! Noah knew the waters were going down. When he sent the dove out a third time, it didn't return – it had found a new home on the dry earth.

When everything was completely dry, God told Noah to leave the ark. Imagine stepping out onto a completely clean, fresh world! The first thing Noah did was build an altar and offer sacrifices to thank God for keeping them safe. God was pleased with Noah's offering and made a special promise – a covenant – with Noah and all future generations. He promised never to flood the entire earth again, and He set a rainbow in the sky as a sign of this promise.

God blessed Noah and his family, telling them to multiply and fill the earth again. He gave them new rules for this new world, including permission to eat meat (before this, humans had been vegetarians). But He also gave them greater responsibility to take care of each other and the animals.

From Noah's three sons came all the nations of the earth. People began to spread out and repopulate the world. While things weren't perfect – Noah's family still made mistakes, as we all do – God had given humanity a fresh start. The flood story teaches us important lessons about God's justice and mercy: He must deal with sin, but He also provides a way to save those who trust and obey Him.

🔍 Time Travel Corner:

Imagine standing in ancient Mesopotamia, where this story was first written down! Archaeologists have found evidence of massive floods in this region, including a layer of mud and debris over 8 feet thick dating back to around 2900 BC. Many ancient civilizations, from the Babylonians to the Greeks, had their own flood stories. The most famous is the Epic of Gilgamesh, which shares some fascinating similarities with Noah's story – but the Bible's account stands unique in its focus on God's justice and mercy rather than quarreling gods.

💡 Did You Know?

- The wood used for the ark was "gopher wood" – though nobody today knows exactly what kind of wood this was!

- The ark was about 1½ times the length of a football field

- Scientists have calculated that the ark would have been perfectly stable on the waters, even in rough seas

- If the average animal was the size of a sheep, the ark could have held over 125,000 animals

- Many of today's ship-building principles match the proportions God gave Noah

💭 Think About It:

1. Why do you think God chose to save animals along with humans?

2. What would it have been like to be Noah, building the ark while everyone laughed?

3. How do you think Noah's family felt during those long days on the ark?

4. What does the rainbow mean to you when you see it today?

5. How can we be like Noah in standing up for what's right, even when others disagree?

Your Turn:

- Design your own ark! Draw a cross-section showing how you would arrange the different animals

- Keep a diary for a week as if you were on the ark

- Research animals that live in your area – how many pairs would you need to save?

- Create a rainfall gauge and track precipitation for a month

Dig Deeper:

Archaeological evidence shows:

- Ancient flood deposits throughout the Middle East

- Remains of early farming communities suddenly abandoned due to flooding

- Studies of the Black Sea revealing evidence of a massive flood

- Ancient Sumerian tablets containing detailed flood accounts

- Marine fossils found on mountaintops worldwide

👤👤👤👤 Family Talk:

- What's the hardest thing you've ever had to do because God (or mom and dad) asked you to?

- How do we show trust in God today?

- What are some ways our family can help take care of God's creation?

- When have you had to stand up for what's right when others disagreed?

Chapter 2:

Abraham's Journey – Following God's Call

Have you ever had to move to a new city? Leave your friends behind? Start fresh somewhere completely different? If you have, you might understand a little bit of what Abraham felt when God called him to leave everything he knew behind. But Abraham's story isn't just about moving – it's about having faith in God's biggest promises, even when they seem impossible.

Our story begins in a city called Ur of the Chaldeans, in what we now call Iraq. It was a wealthy city with tall buildings, busy markets, and temples reaching toward the sky. People there worshipped many different gods, but Abraham (who was called Abram back then) was different. He believed in the one true God, and that made him special.

One day, when Abram was already seventy-five years old, God spoke to him with an extraordinary request: "Leave your country, your people, and your father's household and go to the land I will show you." But this wasn't just a command – it came with amazing promises.

19

God told Abram, "I will make you into a great nation, and I will bless you. I will make your name great, and you will be a blessing. I will bless those who bless you, and whoever curses you I will curse. Through you, all peoples on earth will be blessed."

Imagine getting those instructions today – it would be like someone telling you to pack up everything and start walking, without even knowing your final destination! There were no maps, no GPS, no phones to call home. The journey would be dangerous, with threats from bandits, wild animals, and harsh weather. Yet Abram didn't hesitate. He packed up everything he owned – his tents, his livestock, and all his possessions. His wife Sarai came with him, along with his nephew Lot and all their servants.

The caravan that left Ur must have been impressive. Abram was already wealthy, with hundreds of servants, large flocks of sheep and goats, herds of cattle, and many camels. As they traveled, their caravan stretched across the landscape like a moving city. They followed the fertile crescent – a curved strip of fertile land that wrapped around the harsh Arabian desert – heading first to Haran, and then south toward Canaan.

The journey wasn't quick or easy. They traveled through deserts where the sun blazed overhead and water was scarce. They crossed rivers where they had to keep their animals from being swept away. They passed through territories controlled by different peoples, some friendly, some not. At night, they would set up their tents under stars so bright and numerous they looked like diamonds scattered across black velvet.

Along the way, whenever they stopped at a significant place, Abram would build an altar to worship God. These altars were more than just piles of stones – they were landmarks of faith, visible reminders that God was guiding their journey. They also showed the local people that Abram worshipped a different God than they did, which wasn't always easy or popular.

When they finally reached Canaan, God appeared to Abram again and said, "To your offspring I will give this land." It must have seemed like an extraordinary promise. The land was already occupied by different groups – the Canaanites and Perizzites lived in cities and controlled the territory. Plus, Abram and Sarai had no children, and they were already quite old. How could their offspring inherit anything if they had no offspring to begin with? But Abram believed God's promise and built another altar there.

As time went on, both Abram and his nephew Lot became even wealthier. Their flocks and herds grew so large that the land couldn't support all their animals grazing together. Their shepherds started arguing over the best pastures and water sources. Abram knew they needed to separate, so he gave Lot first choice of where to live. Looking down from the hills, they could see the whole land spread out before them.

Lot chose what looked like the best option – the fertile Jordan Valley, which was well-watered everywhere, "like the garden of the Lord." He moved his family and flocks near the city of Sodom, where the green valleys promised easy living. Abram took the less attractive option, staying in the hill country of Canaan. But after Lot left, God spoke to Abram again with an even bigger promise: "Look around you – look north, south, east, and west. All the land you see, I will give to you and your offspring forever. And I will make your offspring like the dust of the earth – so numerous that they cannot be counted!"

Still, there was one big problem: Abram and Sarai remained childless. As the years passed, it seemed less and less likely they would ever have a child of their own. Sarai decided to take matters into her own hands. Following the customs of their time, she gave her Egyptian servant Hagar to Abram as a second wife, hoping to build a family through her. Hagar did have a son, whom they named Ishmael. But this wasn't God's plan for fulfilling His promise.

When Abram was ninety-nine years old, God appeared to him again. This time, God changed his name from Abram ("exalted father") to Abraham ("father of many"). He also changed Sarai's name to Sarah, and made an astonishing promise: within a year, Sarah herself would have a son. Abraham laughed at first – after all, he was almost a hundred years old, and Sarah was ninety!

But God was serious. He established a covenant with Abraham, marking him and all his male descendants through circumcision as a sign of this special relationship.

True to His word, God did the impossible. Sarah had a baby boy exactly when God had promised. They named him Isaac, which means "laughter" – a reminder of how they had both laughed in disbelief when God said they would have a child in their old age. Now their laughter was one of pure joy. Isaac was the son they had waited for their entire lives, the one through whom God would fulfill His promises.

But the greatest test of Abraham's faith was still to come. When Isaac was a young boy, God asked Abraham to do something unthinkable: "Take your son, your only son Isaac, whom you love, and go to the region of Moriah. Sacrifice him there as a burnt offering on a mountain I will show you."

Try to imagine how Abraham felt that night. Isaac was the son of the promise, the one God had said would be the father of many nations More than that, he was Abraham's beloved son. The command must have torn at Abraham's heart. Yet early the next morning, Abraham got up, saddled his donkey, and set out with Isaac and two servants. He even carried the wood for the sacrifice.

For three days they traveled. When they reached the mountain, Abraham told the servants to wait while he and Isaac went to worship. Isaac carried the wood while Abraham carried the fire and the knife. As they walked together, Isaac asked the heart-breaking question: "Father, we have the fire and the wood, but where is the lamb for the burnt offering?"

Abraham's response showed his deep faith: "God himself will provide the lamb for the burnt offering, my son." Even in this terrible moment, Abraham trusted that God would somehow keep His promises.

When they reached the place God had chosen, Abraham built an altar and arranged the wood. With trembling hands, he bound Isaac and laid him on the altar. Just as Abraham reached for the knife, the angel of the Lord called out from heaven: "Abraham! Abraham! Do not lay a hand on the boy! Now I know that you fear God, because you have not withheld from me your son, your only son."

Abraham looked up and saw a ram caught by its horns in a thicket. God had indeed provided the sacrifice, just as Abraham had said He would. Abraham offered the ram instead of his son, and named that place "The Lord Will Provide."

Because of Abraham's complete trust and obedience, God renewed His covenant with even greater promises. Abraham's descendants would be as numerous as the stars in the sky and the sand on the seashore. Through his offspring, all nations on earth would be blessed - a promise that would ultimately be fulfilled through Jesus Christ, Abraham's most important descendant.

Abraham lived to be 175 years old. He saw Isaac grow up and marry Rebekah, and lived long enough to see his grandchildren. When he died, he was buried beside Sarah in the cave of Machpelah, the only piece of the Promised Land he ever actually owned. But his legacy lived on through Isaac, and continues today through all who follow his example of faith.

🔍 Time Travel Corner:

Imagine living in ancient Ur, Abraham's hometown! Archaeologists have uncovered amazing things about this city. It had paved streets, two-story houses, and a huge ziggurat (temple tower) that rose about 70 feet high. People there were skilled in mathematics, astronomy, and trading. They wrote on clay tablets using cuneiform writing, and many of these tablets still exist today. The journey Abraham took would have followed the Fertile Crescent, a curved path of fertile land that went up through modern-day Iraq, Syria, and down through Israel.

💡 Did You Know?

- Ur was one of the largest cities in the world at the time, with around 65,000 people

- Abraham's journey from Ur to Canaan was about 1,000 miles long

- Camels could carry up to 400 pounds of cargo each

- The cave of Machpelah where Abraham was buried can still be visited today

- People in Ur had indoor plumbing and complex legal systems

- Abraham's story is important to three major world religions: Judaism, Christianity, and Islam

🧠 Think About It:

1. Why do you think God asked Abraham to leave his comfortable life in Ur?

2. How hard would it be to trust God if He asked you to move somewhere without telling you where?

3. What made Abraham's faith so special that God chose him?

4. How do you think Isaac felt during the sacrifice story?

5. What does this story teach us about trusting God even when things seem impossible?

✏️ Your Turn:

- Draw a map of Abraham's journey using a modern map as reference

- Pack a theoretical "suitcase" for a journey like Abraham's – what would you take?

- Write a diary entry as if you were Isaac on the mountain with Abraham

- Create a family tree showing Abraham's descendants

- Design your own altar like the ones Abraham built

⌖ Dig Deeper: Archaeological discoveries tell us:

- Houses in Ur had 10-12 rooms and were well-designed

- Trade records show the types of goods and animals Abraham might have owned

- Ancient roads and trade routes Abraham likely followed still exist

- Evidence of the types of altars people built during this time

- Remains of ancient wells where travelers like Abraham would have stopped

👤👤👤👤 Family Talk:

- When have you had to trust God with something really important to you?

- What promises has God made to our family? How do we show we trust Him?

- How can we follow Abraham's example of obedience in our daily lives?

- What would you find hardest about leaving everything behind like Abraham did?

- How does God test our faith today, and how can we prepare for those tests?

Chapter 3:

Joseph - From Prisoner to Prince

Have you ever felt like everyone was against you? Like things just kept getting worse no matter what you did? If so, you might understand how Joseph felt during much of his early life. But his story shows us how God can turn the worst situations into something amazing – if we keep trusting Him.

Joseph's story begins with a teenager who had everything going for him. He was the favorite son of his wealthy father, Jacob. As the first son of Rachel, the wife Jacob loved most, Joseph held a special place in his father's heart. Jacob even gave him an expensive, colorful coat – probably something like a designer jacket today. But being the favorite isn't always easy, especially when you have eleven brothers!

To make matters worse, Joseph had vivid dreams that seemed to suggest he would one day rule over his whole family. In one dream, he and his brothers were binding sheaves of grain in the field when suddenly his sheaf stood upright, and his brothers' sheaves bowed down to his. In another dream, the sun, moon, and eleven stars bowed down to him. When he told his family about these dreams, his brothers became even more furious with him. Even his father scolded him, asking, "What is this dream you had? Will your mother and I and your brothers actually come and bow down to the ground before you?"

Joseph's brothers already resented him for being their father's favorite. Now, hearing about these dreams pushed them over the edge. They started plotting against him, looking for a way to get rid of their annoying little brother. Their chance came when Jacob sent Joseph to check on them while they were grazing the flocks far from home.

When Joseph's brothers saw him coming across the fields, wearing his fancy coat, their hatred boiled over. "Here comes that dreamer!" they said to each other. Their first plan was to kill him and throw him into a pit, telling their father that a wild animal had eaten him. But Reuben, the oldest brother, suggested they just throw Joseph into a dry cistern instead, secretly planning to rescue him later.

The brothers stripped Joseph of his special coat and threw him into the deep pit. Imagine how terrified Joseph must have been – trapped in a dark hole, hearing his brothers laughing and eating lunch above him, not knowing what would happen next. But their plan changed when a caravan of Ishmaelite traders passed by on their way to Egypt. Judah, one of the brothers, had an idea: "What will we gain if we kill our brother? Let's sell him to these traders instead."

They pulled Joseph out of the pit and sold him – their own brother – for twenty pieces of silver. The traders bound his hands and forced him to walk behind their camels as they headed for Egypt. To cover up their cruel deed, the brothers dipped Joseph's beautiful coat in goat's blood and brought it to their father. "We found this," they said. "Examine it to see whether it is your son's robe." Jacob recognized it immediately and assumed a wild animal had killed his beloved son. He was inconsolable, refusing to be comforted by any of his children.

Meanwhile, Joseph arrived in Egypt, a land completely foreign to him. Everything was different – the language, the customs, even the way people dressed. The traders sold him to Potiphar, an important Egyptian official who served as captain of Pharaoh's guard. But even in slavery, Joseph's character shone through. He worked hard and showed such wisdom that Potiphar soon put him in charge of his entire household.

Just when things seemed to be looking up, disaster struck again. Potiphar's wife took notice of Joseph, who had grown into a handsome young man. Day after day, she tried to seduce him, but Joseph repeatedly refused, saying, "How could I do such a wicked thing and sin against God?" Finally, one day when they were alone in the house, she grabbed his cloak as he ran away from her. Furious at being rejected, she used his cloak as evidence to falsely accuse him of attempted assault. Potiphar was enraged and had Joseph thrown into prison.

But even in prison, Joseph's integrity and abilities couldn't be hidden. The prison warden soon put him in charge of all the other prisoners. Among them were Pharaoh's chief cupbearer and chief baker, who both had dreams they couldn't understand. Joseph interpreted their dreams correctly: the cupbearer would be restored to his position, but the baker would be executed. Before the cupbearer left, Joseph begged him, "Remember me when it goes well with you. Mention me to Pharaoh and get me out of this prison." But the cupbearer forgot all about Joseph as soon as he was released.

Two full years passed. Joseph remained in prison, perhaps wondering if God had forgotten him too. Then one night, Pharaoh himself had two troubling dreams that none of his wise men could interpret. The cupbearer finally remembered Joseph and told Pharaoh about the young Hebrew prisoner who could interpret dreams. Pharaoh immediately sent for Joseph.

After cleaning up and shaving in the Egyptian style, Joseph was brought before Pharaoh. Imagine stepping into the most magnificent palace you've ever seen, facing the most powerful man in the world. But Joseph remained humble, saying, "I cannot interpret dreams, but God will give Pharaoh the answer he desires."

Pharaoh described his dreams: In the first, seven fat, healthy cows came up from the Nile to graze, followed by seven ugly, thin cows that ate up the healthy ones. In the second dream, seven plump heads of grain were swallowed up by seven thin, scorched heads. Joseph explained that God was showing Pharaoh what was about to happen. Both dreams meant the same thing: Egypt would have seven years of abundance followed by seven years of severe famine.

Then Joseph did something bold – he didn't just interpret the dreams, he proposed a solution: "Choose a wise man to oversee the land. During the seven good years, collect one-fifth of all the grain and store it up. This food will be needed during the seven years of famine that will follow."

Pharaoh was so impressed that he said to his officials, "Can we find anyone like this man, one in whom is the spirit of God?" Then, in an amazing turn of events, Pharaoh appointed Joseph himself as second-in-command over all Egypt. In a single day, Joseph went from being a prisoner to becoming the most powerful man in Egypt after Pharaoh. He was given Pharaoh's own ring, fine linen clothes, and a gold chain. He rode in a chariot as people bowed before him. Pharaoh even gave him an Egyptian name, Zaphenath-Paneah, and arranged his marriage to Asenath, daughter of an important priest.

Joseph was thirty years old when he entered Pharaoh's service – thirteen years after his brothers had sold him into slavery. During the seven years of abundance, he traveled throughout Egypt, building storehouses and collecting grain. He stored up so much that they stopped keeping records because it was beyond measuring. During this time, his wife bore him two sons: Manasseh ("God has made me forget all my trouble") and Ephraim ("God has made me fruitful in the land of my suffering").

When the seven years of plenty ended, the famine began just as God had shown. It affected not just Egypt but all the surrounding lands. While other nations began to starve, Egypt had plenty of food because of Joseph's wise planning. People from all countries came to Egypt to buy grain from Joseph.

Eventually, the famine reached Canaan, where Joseph's family still lived. Jacob sent his sons – all except Benjamin, Joseph's youngest brother – to Egypt to buy food. When the brothers arrived and came before Joseph, they bowed down to him with their faces to the ground, just as his dreams had predicted so many years before. Joseph recognized them immediately, but they didn't recognize this powerful Egyptian ruler as their brother they had sold into slavery so long ago.

Joseph decided to test his brothers to see if they had changed. Speaking harshly through an interpreter, he accused them of being spies. He kept one brother, Simeon, in prison and sent the others home with grain – but secretly returned their payment in their sacks. He also demanded they bring their youngest brother Benjamin next time to prove they were telling the truth.

When the brothers discovered the money in their sacks, they were terrified. Jacob was devastated at the thought of sending Benjamin to Egypt, but when the grain ran out, they had no choice. This time, Joseph invited them all to a feast at his house. When he saw Benjamin, he was so overcome with emotion that he had to leave the room to cry.

Still testing them, Joseph had his silver cup planted in Benjamin's sack and accused him of theft. When the cup was found, he declared that Benjamin must remain as his slave. That's when Judah stepped forward, offering himself in Benjamin's place. He explained how their father had already lost one beloved son and wouldn't survive losing Benjamin too. This selfless act – so different from when they had sold Joseph – showed Joseph that his brothers had truly changed.

Unable to control his emotions any longer, Joseph ordered everyone else out of the room. Then he revealed his identity to his brothers, weeping so loudly that the Egyptians heard him. "I am Joseph!" he declared. "Is my father still living?" His brothers were terrified, but Joseph told them, "Don't be afraid. What you meant for evil, God meant for good, to accomplish what is now being done, the saving of many lives."

Joseph sent his brothers home with wagons full of gifts and food, asking them to bring their father and all their families to Egypt. When Jacob heard that Joseph was alive, he could hardly believe it. But seeing the wagons Joseph had sent convinced him. "I'm convinced!" he said. "My son Joseph is still alive. I will go and see him before I die."

The family's reunion was joyful beyond words. Jacob lived his final seventeen years in Egypt, near Joseph. Before he died, he blessed Joseph's sons, Manasseh and Ephraim, adopting them as his own. Joseph lived to see his great-grandchildren. When he was 110 years old, he made his brothers promise to carry his bones back to Canaan when God eventually led them out of Egypt.

Joseph's story shows how God can work through even the worst circumstances to accomplish His purposes. What looked like disaster – being sold as a slave, being falsely accused, being forgotten in prison – was actually part of God's plan to save not only Joseph's family but many other people as well.

🔍 Time Travel Corner:

Step into ancient Egypt during Joseph's time! This was during the Middle Kingdom period, around 1800 BC. Egypt was at its height of power and sophistication. The Pharaohs lived in magnificent palaces along the Nile River. They built massive grain storage facilities – archaeologists have found remains of these round grain silos that could hold tons of grain. Egyptians were masters of record-keeping, writing everything down on papyrus scrolls using hieroglyphics. They even had a special title for officials like Joseph: "Vizier" – the person who managed the kingdom's resources.

💡 Did You Know?

- Egyptian officials wore special rings called seal

rings to stamp important documents

- The Egyptians were expert grain storers and had developed ways to prevent spoilage

- Dreams were considered very important messages in ancient Egyptian culture

- Egyptians kept careful records of Nile water levels to predict good and bad harvests

- Being clean-shaven was a mark of Egyptian nobility – that's why Joseph had to shave before meeting Pharaoh

- The journey from Canaan to Egypt would have taken Joseph's brothers about three weeks

Think About It:

1. Why do you think Joseph's brothers were so jealous of him at first?

2. How did Joseph stay faithful to God even when everything seemed to go wrong?

3. Why did Joseph test his brothers instead of revealing himself right away?

4. What would you have done in Joseph's place when you saw your brothers again?

5. How can we trust God's plan even when bad things happen to us?

Your Turn:

- Create a timeline of Joseph's life showing all the major events

- Design an Egyptian-style grain storage system

- Write a diary entry as Joseph on the day he became second-in-command

- Draw what you think Joseph's famous coat looked like

- Make a map showing the journey from Canaan to Egypt

Dig Deeper:

Archaeological findings show:

- Evidence of a massive famine during this period in Egyptian history

- Ancient Egyptian grain silos and storage systems

- Remains of the kind of prisons where Joseph would have been held

- Records of foreign officials rising to power in Egypt

- Artifacts showing the type of clothing and jewelry Joseph would have worn

Family Talk:

- Have you ever been treated unfairly? How did you handle it?

- When have you had to forgive someone who hurt you?

- How can we look for God's plan even in difficult situations?

- What can our family learn from how Joseph treated his brothers?

- How can we show trust in God like Joseph did?

Chapter 4:

Moses - The Great Deliverer

Have you ever felt too scared or unsure to do something important? Or maybe you thought you weren't good enough for a big task? If so, you'll understand exactly how Moses felt when God called him to lead an entire nation to freedom. His story shows us that God doesn't always choose the people we might expect – and that with God's help, ordinary people can do extraordinary things.

Our story begins during a dark time for the Israelites. Joseph had died long ago, and a new Pharaoh ruled Egypt who didn't remember how Joseph had saved the country. The Israelites (also called Hebrews) had grown from just a large family into a whole nation of people. The new Pharaoh was afraid they were becoming too numerous and powerful, so he turned them into slaves. He forced them to make bricks, build cities, and work in the fields under cruel slave drivers who beat them and treated them terribly.

But the Israelites kept growing in number, so Pharaoh made an awful decision: every Hebrew baby boy was to be thrown into the Nile River to drown. It was during this dangerous time that a Levite woman gave birth to a beautiful baby boy. For three months, she managed to hide him. But when she couldn't hide him any longer, she made a waterproof basket from papyrus reeds, placed her baby inside, and set it among the tall grass at the edge of the Nile River. The baby's sister, Miriam, stayed nearby to watch what would happen.

What happened next could only have been arranged by God: Pharaoh's own daughter came down to bathe in the river. When she saw the basket, she sent her servant to get it. Opening it, she found the crying baby and felt sorry for him. "This is one of the Hebrew babies," she said. That's when Miriam bravely stepped forward and offered to find a Hebrew woman to nurse the child. Of course, she went and got the baby's own mother!

Pharaoh's daughter adopted the baby as her own son and named him Moses, which means "drawn out of the water." So Moses grew up in the palace as an Egyptian prince, but he was nursed and taught by his own Hebrew mother. Imagine living this double life – enjoying all the luxuries of the palace while knowing your real family and people were suffering as slaves.

The Bible tells us Moses was educated in all the wisdom of the Egyptians. He would have learned to read and write hieroglyphics, studied mathematics and architecture, learned about Egyptian religion and law, and trained in military strategy. He grew into a powerful and respected man in Egypt. But he never forgot who he really was – a Hebrew.

One day, when Moses was forty years old, he went out to watch his people working as slaves. He saw an Egyptian beating a Hebrew slave. Looking around to make sure no one was watching, Moses killed the Egyptian and buried him in the sand. The next day, he saw two Hebrew men fighting. When he tried to stop them, one of them said, "Who made you ruler and judge over us? Are you going to kill me as you killed the Egyptian?"

Moses realized his secret wasn't safe. When Pharaoh heard about what happened, he tried to kill Moses. Suddenly, the prince of Egypt became a wanted man. Moses fled into the desert, traveling all the way to a place called Midian. There, he sat down by a well – tired, thirsty, and probably wondering how his life had gone so wrong so quickly.

While he was there, seven sisters came to water their father's flocks. Some shepherds tried to drive them away, but Moses stood up and helped the women. This led to Moses meeting their father, Reuel (also called Jethro), who was a priest of Midian. Moses ended up staying with this family, marrying one of the daughters, Zipporah, and becoming a shepherd.

What a change in life! From living in palaces and wearing fine clothes, Moses now lived in tents and spent his days watching sheep in the wilderness. For forty years, he lived this quiet life. He and Zipporah had two sons, and he might have thought his days of adventure were over. But God had other plans.

One ordinary day, while Moses was tending his father-in-law's sheep near Mount Horeb (also called Mount Sinai), he saw something strange: a bush was on fire, but it wasn't burning up. When he went closer to look, God called to him from within the bush: "Moses! Moses!"

"Here I am," Moses replied, not yet realizing he was talking to God. Then came the command: "Do not come any closer. Take off your sandals, for the place where you are standing is holy ground." God introduced Himself as the God of Abraham, Isaac, and Jacob – the God of Moses's ancestors. Moses hid his face, afraid to look at God.

Then God revealed His plan: "I have indeed seen the misery of my people in Egypt. I have heard them crying out because of their slave drivers, and I am concerned about their suffering. So I have come down to rescue them from the hand of the Egyptians and to bring them up out of that land into a good and spacious land, a land flowing with milk and honey. And I am sending you to Pharaoh to bring my people out of Egypt."

Moses couldn't believe his ears. "Who am I that I should go to Pharaoh and bring the Israelites out of Egypt?" he protested. The confident prince had become a humble shepherd, and he didn't feel qualified for such a huge task. But God promised, "I will be with you."

Still, Moses had more objections. "What if they ask me your name? What should I tell them?" God replied with one of the most important revelations in the Bible: "I AM

WHO I AM. Tell them I AM has sent you." This name showed that God is eternal, self-existent, and always present with His people.

But Moses wasn't finished with his excuses. "What if they don't believe me?" he asked. So God gave him three miraculous signs he could perform: his staff could turn into a snake and back again, his hand could become leprous and be healed, and he could turn water from the Nile into blood.

Finally, Moses brought up his biggest worry: "O Lord, I have never been eloquent... I am slow of speech and tongue." Even after God promised to help him speak, Moses begged, "Please send someone else." This made God angry, but He agreed to let Moses's brother Aaron be his spokesman.

Armed with his staff and God's promises, Moses said goodbye to Jethro and headed back to Egypt with his wife and sons. On the way, God warned him that Pharaoh wouldn't let the people go easily, but God would perform mighty wonders to convince him.

When Moses and Aaron arrived in Egypt, they first met with the Israelite elders. When the people saw the miraculous signs and heard that God had seen their misery, they bowed down and worshiped. After four hundred years of slavery, hope was finally rising among God's people.

But when Moses and Aaron went to Pharaoh with God's message – "Let my people go" – things got worse instead of better. Pharaoh not only refused but punished the Israelites by making their work harder. Now they had to gather their own straw to make bricks while still producing the same number as before. The people blamed Moses for making their lives more difficult.

This began an epic confrontation between God and Pharaoh, with Moses and Aaron delivering God's messages. Each time Pharaoh refused to let the people go, God sent another plague on Egypt. First, the Nile turned to blood. Then came plagues of frogs, gnats, and flies. Next, all the Egyptian livestock died, followed by painful boils on people and animals. Then came devastating hail, locusts that ate everything green, and three days of total darkness.

After each plague, Pharaoh would either promise to let the people go and then change his mind, or simply refuse outright. His heart grew harder and harder. Sometimes he tried to compromise, saying they could worship God in Egypt, or the men could go but not the women and children. But Moses insisted that everyone must go, along with all their livestock.

Finally, God announced the last and most terrible plague: every firstborn son in Egypt would die, from Pharaoh's son to the son of the lowliest slave. But God provided a way for the Israelites to be saved. Each family was to sacrifice a perfect lamb and put its blood on the doorposts of their house. When the angel of death came through Egypt, it would "pass over" the houses with blood on the doorposts.

That night, the Israelites ate a special meal of roasted lamb, bitter herbs, and bread made without yeast, ready to leave at a moment's notice. At midnight, a great cry went up across Egypt as every Egyptian household lost their firstborn son. But all the Israelite homes with blood on their doorposts were safe.

Finally, Pharaoh had had enough. He summoned Moses and Aaron in the night and told them to take all the Israelites and their flocks and leave Egypt immediately. The Egyptians urged them to hurry, even giving them gold, silver, and clothing just to get them to go quickly. After 430 years in Egypt, the Israelites – now numbering about 600,000 men, plus women and children – set out for freedom.

God led them with a pillar of cloud by day and a pillar of fire by night. But their journey had only begun. When Pharaoh realized his workforce had left, he changed his mind one final time. He gathered his army and chariots and chased after the Israelites, trapping them between his army and the Red Sea.

The people were terrified, but Moses told them, "Stand firm and you will see the deliverance the Lord will bring you today... The Lord will fight for you; you need only to be still." Then God did something amazing: He made the pillar of cloud move between the Israelites and the Egyptian army. Then Moses stretched out his staff over the sea, and God sent a strong east wind that parted the waters, creating a dry path through the sea with walls of water on both sides

All night long, the Israelites walked through the sea on dry ground, with walls of water on their right and left. When morning came, Pharaoh's army followed them into the sea. But God threw the Egyptian army into confusion, making their chariot wheels stick and fall off. The Egyptians realized God was fighting for the Israelites and tried to retreat, but it was too late. Moses stretched out his hand again, and the waters crashed back together, drowning the entire Egyptian army.

When the Israelites saw what had happened, they were filled with awe. They trusted in God and in Moses, His servant. Moses's sister Miriam led all the women in a victory dance with tambourines, singing, "Sing to the Lord, for he is highly exalted. Both horse and driver he has hurled into the sea!"

This incredible rescue became the defining moment in Israel's history. Year after year, they would celebrate the Passover to remember how God had delivered them from slavery. The story would be told to children and grandchildren, reminding them that God keeps His promises and fights for His people.

Moses would go on to lead the people through many more challenges in the wilderness, receiving the Ten Commandments, establishing God's laws, and dealing with the people's complaints and rebellion. Though he wouldn't live to enter the Promised Land himself, he had fulfilled his role as God's chosen deliverer, turning from a hesitant shepherd into one of the greatest leaders in history.

🔍 Time Travel Corner:

Welcome to ancient Egypt around 1446 BC! Archaeological evidence shows that Egypt was at the height of its power during this time, under the 18th Dynasty. The city where Moses grew up would have had magnificent temples, towering obelisks, and bustling markets. Egyptians used advanced engineering to build with stone, created incredible art, and developed complex irrigation systems along the Nile. As a prince, Moses would have lived in a palace with painted walls, eaten from golden plates, and studied in the world's most advanced civilization of its time.

💡 Did You Know?

- Egyptian princes learned to read and write over 700 hieroglyphic symbols

- The route of the Exodus can still be traced through archaeological sites today

- Making bricks with straw made them stronger by binding the clay together

- Shepherds were considered unclean by Egyptians, showing how much Moses gave up

- The crossing point of the Red Sea was likely near modern-day Gulf of Suez

- Some of the plagues directly challenged specific Egyptian gods

💭 Think About It:

1. Why do you think God chose someone who didn't want the job?

2. How did Moses's palace education and shepherd experience both prepare him?

3. Why did God send ten plagues instead of just one big one?

4. What would it have felt like walking through the Red Sea?

5. How can we be brave like Moses when God gives us hard tasks?

🔎 Your Turn:

- Draw a map of Moses's journey from the palace to Midian to Egypt again

- Design what you think the burning bush looked like

- Create a comic strip showing the ten plagues

- Write a diary entry as an Israelite crossing the Red Sea

- Make a timeline of Moses's life showing his major turning points

↖ Dig Deeper:

Archaeological discoveries show:

- Egyptian chariot remains in the Red Sea area

- Ancient Egyptian buildings made with the same type of bricks described in Exodus

- Evidence of catastrophic events that could correlate with the plagues

- Ancient Egyptian documents mentioning Semitic slaves

- Midianite settlements where Moses might have lived

👤👤👤👤 Family Talk:

- When have you felt too scared or unsure to do something important?

- How has God helped our family through difficult times?

- What excuses do we make when we don't want to do something hard?

- How can we trust God like Moses did when things look impossible?

- What "Red Seas" are we facing that we need God's help to get through?

Chapter 5:

David - From Shepherd to King

Have you ever felt like everyone thinks you're too young or too small to do something important? Maybe your older siblings tell you you're not big enough to play with them, or adults say you're too young to help with big tasks. If so, you'll understand exactly how David felt when he faced the giant Goliath. His story shows us that God doesn't look at age, size, or strength the way people do – He looks at the heart.

Our story begins when David was just a young shepherd boy, probably around your age. While his older brothers were off fighting in King Saul's army, David spent his days taking care of his father's sheep in the hills around Bethlehem. This might sound like a boring job, but it was actually quite dangerous. David had to protect his sheep from lions and bears, and he became very skilled with his shepherd's staff and his sling.

But there was another side to David. During those long hours watching the sheep, he composed songs about God, playing them on his harp. These songs, many of which became psalms in the Bible, showed David's deep love for God and his trust in God's protection. Little did he know that both his courage as a shepherd and his musical abilities would soon play important roles in God's plan for his life.

At this time, Israel was at war with their enemies, the Philistines. The two armies faced each other across a valley, with each camping on a hillside. Every day, a giant Philistine warrior named Goliath would stride into the valley and challenge the Israelites to send someone to fight him. Goliath was over nine feet tall, wore heavy bronze armor, and carried enormous weapons. His very appearance terrified the Israelite army, and no one dared to fight him.

One day, David's father Jesse asked him to take some food to his three oldest brothers who were serving in Saul's army. When David arrived at the camp early in the morning, he heard Goliath shouting his usual challenge: "Why do you come out and line up for battle? Choose a man and have him come down to me. If he fights and kills me, we will become your subjects; but if I overcome him and kill him, you will become our subjects and serve us!"

David watched as the Israelite soldiers ran away in fear. He started asking questions about this giant who dared to insult God's army. His oldest brother Eliab heard him talking and became angry. "Why have you come down here? And with whom did you leave those few sheep in the wilderness? I know how conceited you are and how wicked your heart is; you came down only to watch the battle!"

But David wouldn't be silenced. He kept asking about Goliath, and soon someone told King Saul about this young shepherd who seemed interested in fighting the giant. When Saul sent for him, David said something remarkable: "Let no one lose heart on account of this Philistine; your servant will go and fight him."

Saul looked at David in disbelief. "You are not able to go out against this Philistine and fight him; you are only a young man, and he has been a warrior from his youth." But David explained how God had helped him protect his sheep: "When a lion or a bear came and carried off a sheep from the flock, I went after it, struck it, and rescued the sheep from its mouth. When it turned on me, I seized it by its hair, struck it, and killed it. The Lord who rescued me from the paw of the lion and the paw of the bear will rescue me from the hand of this Philistine."

Saul was impressed by David's confidence but still worried about sending such a young person against Goliath. He tried to give David his own armor to wear – a bronze helmet, a coat of mail, and his sword. David put them on but could hardly walk. "I cannot go in these," he said, "because I am not used to them." Instead, he took them off and picked up his staff, his sling, and chose five smooth stones from a nearby stream.

When Goliath saw David coming toward him, he was insulted. Here was this good-looking young boy with no armor, carrying just a staff like he was going to walk his dog! "Am I a dog, that you come at me with sticks?"

Goliath roared. He cursed David by his gods and shouted, "Come here, and I'll give your flesh to the birds and the wild animals!"

But David's response showed where his confidence really came from: "You come against me with sword and spear and javelin, but I come against you in the name of the Lord Almighty, the God of the armies of Israel, whom you have defied. This day the Lord will deliver you into my hands... and the whole world will know that there is a God in Israel. All those gathered here will know that it is not by sword or spear that the Lord saves; for the battle is the Lord's, and he will give all of you into our hands."

As Goliath moved toward him, David ran quickly to meet him. He reached into his bag, took out a stone, and placed it in his sling. With practiced skill from years of protecting his sheep, he slung it at Goliath. The stone struck the giant in the forehead with such force that it sank into his skull, and he fell face down on the ground. David hadn't even needed the other four stones!

Without a sword of his own, David ran and stood over the giant, grabbed Goliath's huge sword, and used it to cut off the giant's head. When the Philistines saw their champion was dead, they turned and ran. The Israelite army, suddenly filled with courage, chased after them with a mighty shout.

King Saul was so impressed that he kept David in his service from that day on. David was given command of soldiers and won battle after battle. He became best friends with Saul's son Jonathan, who gave David his own robe, armor, sword, bow, and belt as a sign of their friendship.

But David's success soon caused problems. When the army would return from battles, the women would come out singing, "Saul has slain his thousands, and David his tens of thousands!" This made King Saul very jealous. He began to watch David with suspicion, wondering if this popular young warrior might try to take his throne.

What Saul didn't know was that God had already chosen David to be the next king. Sometime before the battle with Goliath, God had sent the prophet Samuel to Bethlehem to anoint one of Jesse's sons as the future king. Samuel had looked at all of David's older brothers, thinking surely one of these strong, tall men must be God's choice. But God told Samuel, "Do not consider his appearance or his height... The Lord does not look at the things people look at. People look at the outward appearance, but the Lord looks at the heart."

Saul's jealousy grew worse and worse. One day, while David was playing the harp to soothe the king's troubled mind (as he often did), Saul suddenly hurled his spear at David, trying to pin him to the wall! David escaped, but he realized his life was in danger. Despite being married to Saul's daughter Michal and being Jonathan's best friend, David had to flee.

For years, David lived as a fugitive. He hid in caves, forests, and wilderness areas, always staying one step ahead of Saul's pursuing army. A group of about 600 men joined him, and David became their leader. Even though he had already been anointed as the next king, and even though Saul was trying to kill him, David refused to harm Saul. Twice he had the chance to kill the king – once when Saul entered a cave where David and his men were hiding, and once when David snuck into Saul's camp at night. Both times, David spared Saul's life, saying, "I will not lay my hand on the Lord's anointed."

Finally, after many years of running, Saul and Jonathan were killed in a battle against the Philistines. When David heard the news, he didn't celebrate his enemy's death. Instead, he wrote a beautiful song of lament, honoring both Saul and Jonathan. Only then did David become king, first over the tribe of Judah, and eventually over all Israel.

David went on to become Israel's greatest king. He captured Jerusalem and made it his capital city. He brought the Ark of the Covenant there, establishing Jerusalem as both the political and religious center of Israel. Under his leadership, Israel grew from a loose confederation of tribes into a powerful kingdom. But more importantly, David was called "a man after God's own heart" because he loved God deeply and tried to follow God's ways, even though he wasn't perfect.

Throughout his life – as a shepherd boy, a giant-slayer, a fugitive, and a king – David never forgot that his strength came from God. Many of the psalms he wrote during these different periods of his life are still used today to express praise, thanksgiving, fear, joy, and trust in God. His victory over Goliath became a lasting symbol that with God's help, even the biggest challenges can be overcome.

🔍 Time Travel Corner:

Welcome to ancient Israel around 1000 BC! Archaeologists have found remains of Philistine cities, including the types of armor and weapons Goliath might have used. A typical Philistine warrior wore bronze scale armor, a helmet, and carried a spear with a shaft like a weaver's beam. The Valley of Elah, where David fought Goliath, can still be visited today. It's a wide valley with smooth stones in its stream – perfect for a shepherd's sling. Skilled slingers of that time could hit targets with the force of a modern handgun!

💡 Did You Know?

- Shepherds' slings were serious weapons, not toys like modern slingshots

- Goliath's armor weighed about 125 pounds

- David's five stones might have been because Goliath had four brothers

- The Valley of Elah was a strategic passage from Philistine territory to Israel's hills

- Archaeological digs have found bronze arrowheads and spearheads from this period

- Jerusalem's ancient City of David can still be visited today

🧠 Think About It:

1. Why did God choose David when everyone else thought his brothers were better choices?

2. How did David's time as a shepherd prepare him for bigger challenges?

3. Why did David refuse to hurt Saul even when Saul was trying to kill him?

4. What made David different from Saul as a king?

5. How can we face our own "giants" with courage like David's?

📣 Your Turn:

- Measure out Goliath's height (about 9'9") compared to your height

- Practice using a sling (safely!) to understand David's skill

- Write your own psalm expressing trust in God like David did

- Draw a map of David's hideouts while running from Saul

- Create a timeline of David's journey from shepherd to king

↖ Dig Deeper:

Archaeological discoveries show:

- Philistine weapons and armor similar to Goliath's description

- Ancient sling stones of the exact size David would have used

- Remains of the ancient city of Gath, Goliath's hometown

- Evidence of David's kingdom in Jerusalem

- Ancient musical instruments like those David would have played

👥👥👥👤 Family Talk:

- What makes you feel small or unimportant sometimes?

- How can our family encourage each other when facing big challenges?

- When have you had to forgive someone who hurt you, like David forgave Saul?

- What talents has God given you that others might not see?

- How can we remember to trust God when we're afraid?

Chapter 6:

Esther - For Such a Time as This

Have you ever had to keep a secret to protect someone? Or needed to be brave even when you were terrified? If so, you'll understand some of what Esther felt when she became queen of Persia and faced the challenge of saving her entire people. Her story shows us how God can place us in exactly the right position to make a difference, even when the situation seems impossible.

Our story begins in the magnificent city of Susa, one of the capitals of the Persian Empire – the largest empire the world had ever seen at that time. King Xerxes ruled over 127 provinces stretching from India to Ethiopia. The king had just banished his queen, Vashti, for refusing to appear at a royal banquet, and his advisors suggested holding a beauty contest to choose a new queen from among all the beautiful young women in the empire.

Among these women was a Jewish girl named Hadassah, though she was better known by her Persian name, Esther. She had been raised by her older cousin Mordecai after her parents died. Esther was beautiful, but she also had a quick mind and a graceful way about her that made people like her. When she was taken to the palace with the other candidates, Mordecai told her not to reveal that she was Jewish, fearing it might put her in danger.

For twelve months, all the women went through extensive beauty treatments – six months with oil of myrrh and six months with special perfumes and cosmetics. During this time, Esther won the favor of Hegai, the king's eunuch in charge of the women. He gave her special beauty treatments and the best place in the harem. When it was Esther's turn to go before the king, she asked for only what Hegai suggested she take. This wisdom paid off – King Xerxes was so impressed with Esther that he chose her as his new queen.

Meanwhile, Mordecai sat at the king's gate each day to hear news of Esther. One day, he overheard two palace guards plotting to assassinate King Xerxes. He told Esther, who warned the king, giving credit to Mordecai. The plot was uncovered, the guards were executed, and the event was written in the king's official records – though Mordecai received no immediate reward.

Around this time, King Xerxes promoted a man named Haman to be his highest official. The king commanded all his officials to bow down to Haman, but Mordecai refused. As a faithful Jew, he would only bow to God. When people asked why he wouldn't bow, Mordecai told them he was Jewish. This made Haman furious. But instead of just punishing Mordecai, Haman's pride and anger led him to plot something far worse – the destruction of all Jewish people throughout the entire Persian Empire.

Haman went to King Xerxes and said, "There is a certain people dispersed among the provinces of your kingdom who keep themselves separate. Their customs are different from those of all other people, and they do not obey your laws. It is not in the king's best interest to tolerate them." Then Haman offered to pay a huge amount of silver into the royal treasury if the king would issue a decree to destroy these people. Not realizing who these people were – or that his own queen was one of them – the king agreed.

Royal scribes wrote the decree and sent it to every province: on a single day, the 13th of the month of Adar, all Jews – including women and children – were to be killed. Their property would be given to those who killed them. The city of Susa was thrown into confusion by this shocking announcement, but Haman and the king sat down to drink together, as if they hadn't just ordered the death of thousands of innocent people.

When Mordecai learned what had happened, he tore his clothes, put on sackcloth and ashes (signs of mourning), and went through the city crying loudly and bitterly. Jews throughout the empire did the same, fasting and weeping when they heard the news. When Esther's servants told her about Mordecai, she sent clothes for him to change into, but he refused them.

Through a messenger, Mordecai sent Esther a copy of the decree and urged her to go to the king and beg for mercy for her people. But Esther sent back a troubling reply: "Everyone knows that anyone who approaches the king in the inner court without being called is doomed to die unless the king extends his gold scepter. And I haven't been called to go to the king for thirty days."

Mordecai's response became one of the most famous passages in the book of Esther: "Don't think that because you live in the king's house you alone of all the Jews will escape. For if you remain silent at this time, relief and deliverance for the Jews will arise from another place, but you and your father's family will perish. And who knows but that you have come to your royal position for such a time as this?"

These words stirred Esther's courage. She sent back her answer: "Go, gather all the Jews who are in Susa, and fast for me. Don't eat or drink for three days, night or day. I and my attendants will fast as you do. Then I will go to the king, even though it is against the law. And if I perish, I perish."

After three days of fasting, Esther put on her royal robes and stood in the inner court of the palace. When the king saw her, he was pleased and held out his golden scepter. Esther approached and touched the tip of the scepter. "What is your request?" the king asked. "Even up to half the kingdom, it will be given you."

But Esther was wise. Instead of making her request immediately, she invited the king and Haman to a special banquet. During the banquet, when the king again asked what she wanted, she invited them to a second banquet the next day, when she would make her request known.

Haman left the first banquet feeling very proud – only he had been invited to dine with the king and queen! But his joy turned to rage when he saw Mordecai, who still refused to bow to him. At his wife's suggestion, Haman built a gallows 75 feet high, planning to ask the king's permission the next morning to hang Mordecai on it.

That night, the king couldn't sleep. He ordered the royal records to be read to him, and learned about how Mordecai had exposed the assassination plot – and had never been rewarded. Early the next morning, Haman came to ask about hanging Mordecai. Before he could speak, the king asked him, "What should be done for the man the king delights to honor?"

Thinking the king meant to honor him, Haman suggested an elaborate parade: the man should wear royal robes the king himself had worn, ride the king's own horse with royal crest, and be led through the city streets by a noble who would proclaim, "This is what is done for the man the king delights to honor!"

"Excellent!" said the king. "Go at once and do exactly this – for Mordecai the Jew!"

Imagine Haman's humiliation as he had to lead Mordecai through the city streets, proclaiming his honor! After this public display, Haman rushed home in shame, only to be immediately summoned to Esther's second banquet.

At this banquet, the king once again asked Esther what she wanted. This time, she revealed her request: "If I have found favor with you, O king, grant me my life – this is my petition. And spare my people – this is my request. For I and my people have been sold for destruction and slaughter and annihilation."

The king was shocked. "Who is he? Where is the man who has dared to do such a thing?"

Esther pointed directly at Haman: "The adversary and enemy is this wicked Haman!"

Haman was terrified. The king, furious, stormed out into the palace garden. When he returned, he found Haman falling on the couch where Esther was reclining, begging for his life. This only made things worse – the king thought Haman was attacking the queen! One of the king's attendants mentioned the tall gallows Haman had built for Mordecai, and the king ordered, "Hang him on it!" So Haman was hanged on the very gallows he had prepared for Mordecai.

But the story wasn't over. The decree to destroy the Jews had been sealed with the king's ring and, according to Persian law, couldn't be reversed. So the king issued a new decree, allowing the Jews to defend themselves against anyone who attacked them. When the dreaded day arrived, the Jews successfully defended themselves throughout the empire. Mordecai was given Haman's position, becoming second only to King Xerxes.

To celebrate their deliverance, the Jews established the festival of Purim, named after the "pur" (lot) that Haman had cast to choose the day for their destruction. Even today, Jewish people celebrate Purim by reading the book of Esther, giving gifts to each other and to the poor, and rejoicing in how God used a brave young woman to save her people.

Through Esther's courage and wisdom, God had once again protected His people. Though God is never directly mentioned in the book of Esther, His providence is clearly seen in every "coincidence" - from Esther becoming queen, to the king's sleepless night, to the timing of every event. Esther's story reminds us that God often works behind the scenes, placing people in positions where they can make a difference if they have the courage to act.

🔍 Time Travel Corner:

Welcome to ancient Persia around 480 BC! The palace at Susa was one of the most magnificent buildings in the ancient world. Archaeologists have uncovered its remains, showing colored glazed bricks, massive columns, and grand staircases. The king's throne room was huge, with walls decorated in gold and precious stones. The Persian Empire was highly organized, with a sophisticated postal system that could deliver messages throughout its vast territory in just days. The king's scribes wrote official documents on clay tablets and parchment scrolls in multiple languages.

💡 Did You Know?

- The Persian Empire covered about 2.9 million square miles

- The palace at Susa had special cooling systems for summer heat

- Persian queens had their own palace buildings and staff

- The royal beauty treatments used expensive spices and oils from across Asia

- Persian kings wore purple robes and special high-heeled shoes

- The empire had a system of roads called the Royal Road, stretching 1,677 miles

🧠 Think About It:

1. Why was it risky for Esther to hide her Jewish identity at first?

2. How did Esther show wisdom in the way she approached the king?

3. What might have happened if Esther had remained silent?

4. How did small "coincidences" add up to save the Jewish people?

5. Where do we see God working behind the scenes in this story?

Your Turn:

- Design a royal Persian robe for Esther

- Create a map showing the size of the Persian Empire

- Write a diary entry from Esther's perspective before approaching the king

- Plan your own Purim celebration

- Draw the palace at Susa based on archaeological descriptions

Dig Deeper:

Archaeological discoveries show:

- Remains of the actual palace where Esther lived

- Ancient Persian royal decrees similar to those in the story

- Evidence of the postal system used to send the king's messages

- Jewelry and cosmetics used by Persian nobility

- Clay tablets describing life in the Persian court

👤👥👤👤 Family Talk:

- When have you needed to be brave to help others?

- How can we recognize when God puts us in the right place at the right time?

- What makes it hard to stand up for what's right?

- How can we support each other when facing difficult decisions?

- What "such a time as this" might God be preparing us for?

Chapter 7:

Daniel - Standing Strong in a Foreign Land

Have you ever felt pressure to do something you knew wasn't right? Maybe your friends were all doing it, or maybe it would have made your life easier to just go along with everyone else. If so, you'll understand the challenges Daniel faced when he was taken far from home to live in Babylon. His story shows us how to stay true to what we believe, even when it's difficult.

Our story begins at a dark time in Israel's history. Jerusalem had been conquered by the powerful Babylonian Empire, and King Nebuchadnezzar ordered that the best and brightest young men from noble Jewish families be brought to Babylon. These young men would be trained to serve in his palace. Among them was Daniel, probably only about fourteen or fifteen years old.

Imagine being taken from everything you knew – your family, your home, your customs – and brought to a strange city with different languages, different gods, and different ways of living. The very name of the city,

Babylon, with its famous hanging gardens and massive ziggurats (temple towers), must have seemed overwhelming to a young person from Jerusalem.

Daniel and his friends were chosen because they were handsome, well-educated, and quick to learn. They were given new Babylonian names: Daniel became Belteshazzar, and his three friends – Hananiah, Mishael, and Azariah – became Shadrach, Meshach, and Abednego. They were to spend three years learning the language and literature of Babylon before entering the king's service.

But Daniel and his friends faced their first challenge right away. The king assigned them special food and wine from his own table – a great honor, but a problem for these young Jews. This food wouldn't have been prepared according to God's laws, and some of it was probably sacrificed to Babylonian idols first. Daniel knew eating this food would be wrong, but refusing the king's food could have been seen as an insult – even rebellion.

Daniel could have made excuses: "I'm far from home, so the rules don't apply," or "I have to do this to survive." Instead, he respectfully asked the chief official for permission not to eat the king's food. He requested that he and his friends be given only vegetables to eat and water to drink for ten days, as a test. "Then compare our appearance with that of the young men who eat the royal food, and treat your servants according to what you see," he suggested.

The official was worried – if Daniel and his friends looked worse than the other young men, the king might have him executed! But Daniel had earned his trust, so he agreed to the test. After ten days, Daniel and his friends looked healthier and better nourished than all the young men who ate the royal food. From then on, they were allowed to continue eating according to their beliefs.

This might seem like a small victory, but it set the pattern for Daniel's entire life. By standing firm in what seemed like a small matter, he and his friends developed the strength they would need for bigger challenges ahead. During their three years of training, God gave them knowledge and understanding of all kinds of literature and learning. To Daniel, He gave the special ability to understand visions and dreams.

When their training was complete, the king questioned them and found them ten times better than all the magicians and enchanters in his whole kingdom. They entered his service, but their biggest tests were still to come.

One night, King Nebuchadnezzar had a dream that troubled him so much he couldn't sleep. He called in all his magicians, enchanters, sorcerers, and astrologers, but made an impossible demand: they had to tell him both what he had dreamed and what it meant. If they couldn't, they would be cut into pieces and their houses turned into piles of rubble. If they could, they would receive rich rewards.

The wise men protested: "No one has ever been asked to do such a thing! Only the gods could know what you dreamed!" This made the king so angry he ordered all the wise men of Babylon to be executed – including Daniel and his friends, even though they hadn't been present for this conversation.

When Daniel learned what was happening, he went to the king and asked for time to interpret the dream. Then he and his friends prayed for God to reveal this mystery. That night, God showed Daniel the dream and its meaning in a vision. Daniel's first response was to praise God: "Praise be to the name of God forever and ever; wisdom and power are his. He gives wisdom to the wise and knowledge to the discerning. He reveals deep and hidden things; he knows what lies in darkness, and light dwells with him."

Then Daniel went to the king and described his dream: The king had seen a huge statue with a head of gold, chest and arms of silver, belly and thighs of bronze, legs of iron, and feet made of iron mixed with clay. Then a rock cut by no human hand struck the statue's feet, destroying it completely. The rock became a huge mountain that filled the whole earth.

Daniel explained that the different parts of the statue represented different kingdoms that would come after Babylon. The head of gold was Nebuchadnezzar's kingdom. After it would come another kingdom (silver), then a third (bronze), and a fourth (iron). The rock represented God's kingdom, which would eventually destroy all earthly kingdoms and last forever.

Instead of being angry at this prediction that his kingdom would fall, Nebuchadnezzar was amazed that Daniel could know his dream. He fell down before Daniel and declared, "Surely your God is the God of gods and the Lord of kings and a revealer of mysteries." He made Daniel ruler over the entire province of Babylon and chief over all his wise men. At Daniel's request, his three friends were also given high positions.

But success brought new challenges. Nebuchadnezzar built a huge golden statue and commanded everyone to bow down and worship it when they heard special music playing. Anyone who refused would be thrown into a blazing furnace. Daniel's three friends – Shadrach, Meshach, and Abednego – refused to bow down, even when the king gave them one last chance.

🔍 Time Travel Corner:

Welcome to ancient Babylon around 600 BC! Archaeologists have uncovered the magnificent city where Daniel lived. The Ishtar Gate, covered in brilliant blue glazed bricks and decorated with golden dragons and bulls, still exists in museums today. Babylon's walls were so thick that chariots could race around the top. The hanging gardens, one of the Seven Wonders of the ancient world, were built on terraces that rose like a mountain. Daniel would have seen students learning mathematics and astronomy in the temple schools, and scribes writing on clay tablets in cuneiform script.

💡 Did You Know?

- Babylon's walls were 56 miles long and wide enough for two chariots to pass

- Young nobles like Daniel had to learn several languages, including Aramaic

- Babylonian astronomers could predict eclipses and track planets

- Lions were kept in the royal menagerie for hunting and entertainment

- The fiery furnace was probably used for smelting metals

- Daniel lived through the reigns of four different kings

💭 Think About It:

1. Why did Daniel take a stand about food but accept his Babylonian name?

2. How did Daniel's early choice about food prepare him for bigger challenges?

3. Why did Daniel keep praying even when he knew about the decree?

4. What made Daniel successful in a foreign culture while staying true to his faith?

5. How can we stand firm in our beliefs when faced with pressure to change?

Your Turn:

- Draw the giant statue from Nebuchadnezzar's dream

- Design a 3D model of the fiery furnace

- Create a timeline of Daniel's life showing major events

- Write a diary entry as Daniel on his first day in Babylon

- Map out the changes in empires during Daniel's lifetime

Dig Deeper: Archaeological discoveries show:

- Remains of Babylon's palace where Daniel served

- Ancient documents describing Babylonian education

- Lion pits used in ancient Mesopotamia

- Babylonian astronomical tablets

- Administrative records from the time period

👤👤👤👤 Family Talk:

- When have you had to stand up for what you believe?

- How can we support each other in making good choices?

- What helps us stay faithful to God when it's difficult?

- How can we be successful in our work/school while keeping our faith?

- What "lions' dens" do we face today?

Chapter 8:

The Greatest Gift - The Birth of Jesus

Have you ever received a gift that you had to wait a very long time for? Something you wanted so much that the waiting seemed almost impossible? The people of Israel had been waiting for hundreds of years for a very special gift – the Messiah, a Savior that God had promised would come. But when He finally arrived, it wasn't in the way anyone expected.

Our story begins in the small town of Nazareth, where a young woman named Mary lived. She was engaged to be married to a carpenter named Joseph, and she was probably busy planning her wedding and dreaming about her future life. But everything changed when God sent the angel Gabriel to visit her.

Imagine how startled Mary must have been when the angel appeared! "Greetings, you who are highly favored! The Lord is with you," Gabriel said. Mary was troubled by his words, wondering what kind of greeting this could be. But the angel continued with an amazing announcement: "Don't be afraid, Mary. You have found favor with God. You will conceive and give birth to a son, and you are to call him Jesus. He will be great and will be called the Son of the Most High. The Lord God will give him the throne of his father David, and his kingdom will never end."

Mary was confused. "How can this be," she asked, "since I am a virgin?" The angel explained that the Holy Spirit would come upon her, and the power of the Most High would overshadow her. The baby would be holy and would be called the Son of God. As a sign, the angel told her that her relative Elizabeth, who was considered too old to have children, was already six months pregnant.

Mary's response showed remarkable faith for someone so young. "I am the Lord's servant," she said. "May your word to me be fulfilled." This wasn't an easy thing to say yes to – being pregnant before marriage could have gotten her rejected by her family, abandoned by Joseph, and even stoned to death according to the law. But Mary trusted God completely.

Joseph, however, hadn't heard from the angel yet. When he found out Mary was pregnant, he was heartbroken. Being a righteous man, he didn't want to expose Mary to public disgrace, so he planned to end their engagement quietly. But then an angel appeared to him in a dream, saying, "Joseph son of David, don't be afraid to take Mary home as your wife, because what is conceived in her is from the Holy Spirit. She will give birth to a son, and you are to give him the name Jesus, because he will save his people from their sins."

When Joseph woke up, he did what the angel commanded and took Mary as his wife. But just as they were settling into life together, a new challenge arose. The Roman emperor, Caesar Augustus, issued a decree that everyone in the empire had to return to their family's hometown to be counted in a census. Since Joseph belonged to the family of David, he had to travel with Mary to Bethlehem, David's city.

It was a difficult journey of about 90 miles from Nazareth to Bethlehem. Mary was in the late stages of her pregnancy, and they probably traveled with a group of other people for safety. The road was rough and dangerous, with steep hills to climb and valleys to cross. They might have walked alongside a donkey carrying their supplies, though the Bible doesn't specifically mention one.

When they finally reached Bethlehem, they found the small town overcrowded with other travelers who had come for the census. Joseph tried to find a place to stay, but every guest room was full. The only space they could find was where animals were kept – perhaps a cave or the lower level of a house where families kept their livestock at night.

It was in this humble place that Mary gave birth to her firstborn son. She wrapped him in strips of cloth called swaddling clothes and laid him in a manger – a feeding trough for animals. The King of kings entered the world not in a palace, but among common farm animals, with the smell of hay and the sounds of cattle nearby.

That same night, in the fields outside Bethlehem, shepherds were watching their flocks. Shepherds were considered among the lowest members of society, often unable to keep all the religious laws because of their work. Yet they were the first to hear the good news. Suddenly, an angel of the Lord appeared to them, and the glory of the Lord shone around them. They were terrified!

"Don't be afraid," the angel said. "I bring you good news that will cause great joy for all the people. Today in the town of David a Savior has been born to you; he is the Messiah, the Lord. This will be a sign to you: You will find a baby wrapped in cloths and lying in a manger."

Then something absolutely spectacular happened – the sky filled with a vast host of angels, praising God and saying, "Glory to God in the highest heaven, and on earth peace to those on whom his favor rests."

When the angels left, the shepherds said to each other, "Let's go to Bethlehem and see this thing that has happened, which the Lord has told us about." They hurried into town and found Mary and Joseph, and the baby lying in the manger. When they saw Jesus, they spread the word about what the angels had told them. Everyone who heard it was amazed.

But this wasn't the end of the remarkable visitors. Far to the east, wise men (also called Magi) had seen a special star rise in the sky. These men studied the stars and ancient writings, and they understood this star meant a new king of the Jews had been born. They packed expensive gifts and set out on a long journey to find this king.

Following the star, they arrived first in Jerusalem, naturally expecting to find a new prince in the capital city. Their questions about the newborn king of the Jews troubled King Herod, who asked the Jewish religious leaders where the Messiah was supposed to be born. They told him the prophecies pointed to Bethlehem.

Herod spoke privately with the wise men and told them to search carefully for the child in Bethlehem. "As soon as you find him," Herod said, "report to me, so that I too may go and worship him." But Herod was lying – he actually planned to kill this potential rival to his throne.

The wise men followed the star to Bethlehem, where it stopped over the place where Jesus was. By this time, Jesus and his family were likely living in a house, not the stable, and he was probably a young toddler. When the wise men saw Jesus with his mother Mary, they bowed down and worshiped him. Then they opened their treasures and presented expensive gifts: gold, frankincense, and myrrh – gifts fit for a king.

But God warned the wise men in a dream not to return to Herod, so they went home by a different route. After they left, an angel appeared to Joseph in a dream: "Get up! Take the child and his mother and escape to Egypt. Stay there until I tell you, for Herod is going to search for the child to kill him."

That very night, Joseph got up, took Jesus and Mary, and left for Egypt. It was just in time – when Herod realized the wise men had outwitted him, he became furious. In his rage, he ordered soldiers to kill all the boys two years old and younger in and around Bethlehem. This horrible act fulfilled another prophecy about Rachel weeping for her children.

Joseph, Mary, and Jesus stayed in Egypt until Herod died. Then another angel appeared to Joseph in a dream, telling him it was safe to return to Israel. But when they heard that Herod's son was ruling in Judea, they went instead to Nazareth in Galilee, where Jesus grew up.

The story of Jesus's birth shows how God works in unexpected ways. The Messiah wasn't born in a palace but in a humble stable. The first announcement wasn't to kings or priests but to lowly shepherds. The family had to become refugees in Egypt, just as the Israelites had been so many centuries before. Yet all of these events fulfilled prophecies written hundreds of years earlier.

Most importantly, this baby was the greatest gift ever given – God Himself coming to earth as a human being to live among us and eventually save us. As the angel had told Joseph, "You are to give him the name Jesus, because he will save his people from their sins."

🔍 Time Travel Corner:

Welcome to first-century Bethlehem! Archaeologists have uncovered what life was like during Jesus's time.

Houses were often two levels, with animals kept on the ground floor at night. Bethlehem was a small town about 5 miles from Jerusalem, sitting on a limestone ridge. The fields where the shepherds watched their flocks were used to raise sheep for temple sacrifices in Jerusalem. The journey from Nazareth to Bethlehem would have taken 4-6 days on foot, traveling about 20 miles per day along ancient trade routes.

💡 Did You Know?

- Swaddling clothes were strips of cloth used to keep babies warm and secure

- The wise men probably arrived up to two years after Jesus's birth

- Frankincense and myrrh were expensive spices used for medicine and worship

- Bethlehem means "house of bread" in Hebrew

- The star might have been visible for months or even years

- Joseph and Mary probably joined a caravan for safety during their journey

💭 Think About It:

1. Why did God choose such humble circumstances for Jesus's birth?

2. How did different people (Mary, Joseph, shepherds, wise men) respond to God's messages?

3. What made the shepherds and wise men leave everything to go see Jesus?

4. Why do you think God warned people through dreams so often in this story?

5. How does Jesus's birth show God's care for all types of people?

Your Turn:

- Draw a map of Mary and Joseph's journey from Nazareth to Bethlehem

- Design the interior of a first-century Bethlehem home

- Create a timeline showing the events from Gabriel's visit to the return from Egypt

- Write a diary entry as one of the shepherds on the night Jesus was born

- Calculate how far the wise men might have traveled to find Jesus

Dig Deeper:

Archaeological discoveries show:

- Remains of first-century homes in Bethlehem

- Ancient trade routes between Nazareth and Bethlehem

- Roman census records and tax documents

- Artifacts showing what daily life was like in Jesus's time

- Evidence of frankincense and myrrh trade routes

👥👥👥👥 Family Talk:

- How do we respond when God asks us to do difficult things?

- What gifts could we give to Jesus today?

- How can we show God's love to people who are often overlooked?

- What makes a gift truly special?

- How can we keep the wonder of Jesus's birth in our hearts all year?

Chapter 9:

Jesus - Walking Among Us

Have you ever wished you could see God face to face? Talk to Him directly and watch Him at work? That's exactly what people got to do when Jesus began His public ministry. For about three years, God Himself walked among people, teaching them, healing them, and showing them what God is really like.

Our story picks up when Jesus was about thirty years old. Until then, He had lived a quiet life in Nazareth, probably working as a carpenter like His earthly father, Joseph. But now it was time for His true mission to begin. He went to the Jordan River, where His cousin John was baptizing people and telling them to prepare for the coming Messiah.

When Jesus asked John to baptize Him, John hesitated. "I need to be baptized by you," he said, "and do you come to me?" But Jesus insisted it was the right thing to do. As Jesus came up out of the water, something amazing happened: the heavens opened, the Holy Spirit descended like a dove, and God's voice spoke from heaven, "This is my Son, whom I love; with Him I am well pleased."

Right after this, the Holy Spirit led Jesus into the wilderness, where He fasted for forty days and faced temptation from Satan. The devil tried to get Jesus to use His power selfishly, to worship him instead of God, and to test God's protection unnecessarily. But Jesus defeated each temptation by quoting Scripture, showing us how to stand firm against temptation ourselves.

After His time in the wilderness, Jesus began gathering followers. Walking by the Sea of Galilee, He saw two fishermen, Simon Peter and his brother Andrew, casting their nets. "Come, follow me," Jesus said, "and I will make you fishers of men." Immediately they left their nets and followed Him. Soon after, He called James and John, who also left their fishing business to follow Him. Eventually, Jesus chose twelve disciples to be His closest followers.

Jesus traveled throughout Galilee, teaching in synagogues and showing people what God's Kingdom was really like. But He didn't just teach – He demonstrated God's power and love through amazing miracles. He turned water into wine at a wedding feast, showing God cares about people's joy. He healed sick people, making the blind see, the lame walk, and even raising the dead. He calmed storms, showing His power over nature. He fed thousands of people with just a few loaves and fish, showing God's ability to provide abundantly.

His teaching was unlike anything people had heard before. Instead of just quoting other teachers, He spoke with His own authority. He often taught using parables –

stories about everyday things that revealed deep spiritual truths. He told stories about farmers planting seeds, women looking for lost coins, shepherds caring for sheep, and fathers welcomng home lost sons. These stories helped people understand what God is like and how He wants us to live.

But what really shocked people was how Jesus treated others. He touched lepers who nobody else would go near. He ate with tax collectors and sinners who were considered outcasts. He showed respect to women and children in a culture that often overlooked them. He even talked to Samaritans, who were enemies of the Jews. Jesus showed that God's love extends to everyone, not just the people others consider worthy.

One day, Jesus climbed a mountain with His disciples and taught them what we now cal the Sermon on the Mount. He explained that God cares about what's in our hearts, not just our outward actions. He taught that true happiness comes from things like being merciful, making peace, and having a pure heart. He told people to love their enemies, pray for those who persecute them, and treat others the way they would want to be treated.

Not everyone was happy about Jesus's growing popularity. The religious leaders of the time – the Pharisees and teachers of the law – became increasingly hostile. They were angry that Jesus claimed to forgive sins (something only God can do), that He didn't follow all their religious rules about the Sabbath, and that He called God His Father, making Himself equal with God.

But Jesus didn't back down. He explained that their religious rules had become more important to them than actually loving God and helping people. He told them they were like whitewashed tombs – clean on the outside but full of dead bones inside. He warned them about being so focused on small rules that they "strained out a gnat but swallowed a camel."

Through it all, Jesus showed who God really is. When a group of children wanted to come to Him, the disciples tried to send them away, but Jesus said, "Let the little children come to me... for the kingdom of heaven belongs to such as these." When a woman caught in adultery was about to be stoned, Jesus challenged her accusers, "Let any one of you who is without sin be the first to throw a stone." When they all left, He told her, "Neither do I condemn you. Go now and leave your life of sin."

Some of Jesus's most powerful teachings came through His miracles. When He healed a paralyzed man lowered through a roof by his friends, He showed both His power to heal and to forgive sins. When He walked on water during a storm, He showed His power over nature and taught Peter about faith. When He raised His friend Lazarus from the dead after four days, He showed His power over death itself and revealed that He is "the resurrection and the life."

Jesus often retreated to quiet places to pray, showing the importance of spending time with God. He taught His disciples to pray what we now call the Lord's Prayer, showing them how to talk to God as a loving Father. He demonstrated servant leadership by washing His disciples' feet, doing the job of the lowest servant.

As His ministry continued, larger and larger crowds followed Him. Once, after He fed five thousand people with just five loaves and two fish, they wanted to make Him king by force. But Jesus explained that He hadn't come to be that kind of king. He told them, "I am the bread of life," explaining that He came to feed their spiritual hunger, not just their physical hunger.

As Jesus's ministry reached its peak, He began telling His disciples that He would go to Jerusalem, suffer many things, be killed, and rise again on the third day. They couldn't understand this – especially Peter, who protested, "Never, Lord! This shall never happen to you!" But Jesus rebuked him, explaining that this was God's plan.

On His way to Jerusalem, Jesus showed more clearly who He was. On a mountain with Peter, James, and John, He was transfigured – His face shone like the sun, and His clothes became as white as light. Moses and Elijah appeared and talked with Him while God's voice again declared, "This is my Son, whom I love. Listen to Him!"

When Jesus entered Jerusalem for the last time, He did so riding on a donkey, fulfilling an ancient prophecy about the Messiah. The crowds welcomed Him like a king, spreading their cloaks on the road and waving palm branches, shouting "Hosanna to the Son of David!" But

Jesus wept over the city, knowing that many would reject Him and that Jerusalem would later be destroyed.

In His final week, Jesus taught daily in the temple courts. He drove out the merchants who had turned the temple into a marketplace, saying, "My house will be called a house of prayer, but you are making it a den of robbers." He told parables warning about judgment coming to those who rejected God's messengers. He spoke about the future, warning His followers about difficult times ahead but promising to return one day.

The night before His death, Jesus shared a final Passover meal with His disciples. He washed their feet, teaching them about serving others. He took bread and wine and gave them new meaning, establishing what we now call Communion or the Lord's Supper. He told them, "This is my body given for you... This cup is the new covenant in my blood."

In all His teachings and actions, Jesus showed that God's kingdom was different from what people expected. It wasn't about political power or religious rules, but about love, service, and transformation of the heart. He taught that the greatest in God's kingdom must be servants of all, and that God's love extends to everyone who will receive it.

🔍 Time Travel Corner:

Welcome to first-century Galilee! Archaeologists have uncovered the remains of fishing villages like Capernaum, where Jesus made His home base. The Sea of Galilee, actually a freshwater lake, was the center of a thriving fishing industry. People traveled on Roman roads connecting various towns, and most spoke both Aramaic and Greek. The countryside was dotted with small farms growing wheat, barley, and olive trees. Synagogues served as community centers where people gathered to study Scripture and discuss community matters.

💡 Did You Know?

- The Sea of Galilee is about 13 miles long and 7 miles wide

- Fishing boats from Jesus's time have been found preserved in the mud

- A typical day's wage was one denarius

- Most houses were made of black basalt stone

- Teachers typically sat while teaching their students

- The temple in Jerusalem was one of the largest religious buildings in the ancient world

💭 Think About It:

1. Why did Jesus often teach using stories about everyday things?

2. How were Jesus's teachings different from what people expected?

3. Why did some people welcome Jesus while others rejected Him?

4. What made Jesus's miracles more than just amazing displays of power?

5. How did Jesus show that God's kingdom is different from earthly kingdoms?

Your Turn:

- Draw a map of Jesus's travels around Galilee

- Write your own parable using modern everyday objects

- Create a timeline of Jesus's three years of ministry

- Design a first-century fishing boat

- List all the different types of people Jesus helped

Dig Deeper:

Archaeological discoveries show

- Peter's house in Capernaum

- Ancient fishing equipment and boats

- Roads Jesus would have walked

- Remains of first-century synagogues

- Tools used by carpenters in Jesus's time

Family Talk:

- Which of Jesus's parables means the most to our family?

- How can we serve others like Jesus did?

- What would it have been like to be one of Jesus's disciples?

- How can we show God's love to people others might ignore?

- What would we ask Jesus if we could spend a day with Him?

Chapter 10:

The Greatest Love - Jesus's Death and Resurrection

Have you ever wondered how far someone would go to show their love for you? Jesus's final days on earth show us the greatest example of love the world has ever seen. But this part of the story starts in a garden, late at night, after Jesus had finished His last supper with His disciples.

In the Garden of Gethsemane, under ancient olive trees, Jesus prayed while His disciples kept falling asleep nearby. He was in such anguish that His sweat was like drops of blood falling to the ground. He knew what was coming - the pain, the shame, the separation from His Father - and He prayed, "Father, if you are willing, take this cup from me; yet not my will, but yours be done." An angel appeared and strengthened Him for what lay ahead.

Suddenly, the quiet garden was filled with noise and torchlight. Judas, one of Jesus's own disciples, led a crowd of soldiers and officials to arrest Him. Judas had agreed to betray Jesus for thirty pieces of silver - the price of a slave. He identified Jesus with a kiss, turning a sign of friendship into a signal for arrest. When Peter tried to defend Jesus with a sword, Jesus stopped him and even healed the ear of the high priest's servant that Peter had cut off.

What followed was a series of unfair trials, starting in the middle of the night. First, they took Jesus to Annas, a former high priest, then to Caiaphas, the current high priest, where the religious leaders had gathered. They brought false witnesses against Him, but their stories didn't match up. Finally, they asked Jesus directly if He was the Son of God. When He said yes, they accused Him of blasphemy.

While this was happening, Peter – who had promised never to deny Jesus – was in the courtyard. Three times people recognized him as one of Jesus's followers, and three times he denied it, just as Jesus had predicted. When the rooster crowed, Peter remembered Jesus's words and went out and wept bitterly.

At dawn, the religious leaders took Jesus to Pilate, the Roman governor, because they didn't have the authority to execute someone. They accused Jesus of claiming to be a king and stirring up the people against Rome. Pilate questioned Jesus and found no basis for the charges, so he sent Him to Herod, who sent Him back to Pilate. Pilate tried to release Jesus, offering to free Him instead of Barabbas, a known criminal. But the crowd, stirred up by the religious leaders, shouted, "Crucify Him!"

Pilate's soldiers mocked Jesus, putting a purple robe on Him and a crown of thorns on His head. They beat Him, spit on Him, and taunted, "Hail, king of the Jews!" Though Pilate still insisted Jesus was innocent, he gave in to the crowd's demands. He washed his hands in front of them, saying, "I am innocent of this man's blood," and handed Jesus over to be crucified.

Jesus was forced to carry His own cross through Jerusalem's streets toward a hill called Golgotha (which means "the place of the skull"). When He was too weak from beatings to carry it anymore, the soldiers made a man named Simon from Cyrene carry it for Him. A large crowd followed, including women who mourned for Him, but Jesus told them, "Don't weep for me; weep for yourselves and for your children."

At Golgotha, they nailed Jesus to the cross between two criminals. Even in His agony, Jesus prayed, "Father, forgive them, for they do not know what they are doing." The soldiers divided His clothes by casting lots, fulfilling an ancient prophecy. Above His head, they placed a sign reading "Jesus of Nazareth, King of the Jews" in three languages.

People passing by hurled insults at Him. "He saved others," they mocked, "but He can't save Himself! Let this Messiah, this king of Israel, come down from the cross, and we will believe in Him." One of the criminals joined in the mocking, but the other rebuked him and said to Jesus, "Remember me when you come into your kingdom." Jesus replied, "Truly I tell you, today you will be with me in paradise."

Near the cross stood Jesus's mother Mary, along with John, His beloved disciple. Looking down at them, Jesus said to His mother, "Woman, here is your son," and to John, "Here is your mother." From that time on, John took Mary into his home.

At noon, darkness came over the whole land for three hours. Then Jesus cried out in a loud voice, "Eli, Eli, lema sabachthani?" which means "My God, my God, why have you forsaken me?" This was the moment when He bore the full weight of humanity's sins, experiencing separation from God so we wouldn't have to.

Shortly after, Jesus said, "I am thirsty." After receiving a drink of wine vinegar, He declared, "It is finished." Then He called out, "Father, into your hands I commit my spirit." With that, He breathed His last.

At that moment, the curtain of the temple was torn in two from top to bottom. The earth shook, rocks split, and tombs broke open. The Roman centurion who had watched everything exclaimed, "Surely this man was the Son of God!"

Because it was nearly the Sabbath, Joseph of Arimathea, a secret follower of Jesus, asked Pilate for permission to take Jesus's body. Along with Nicodemus, another secret disciple, they quickly wrapped Jesus's body with spices in strips of linen and placed it in a new tomb cut out of rock. They rolled a huge stone across the entrance, while some women who had followed Jesus watched where He was laid.

The next day, the religious leaders convinced Pilate to put a guard at the tomb and seal it, remembering that Jesus had said He would rise after three days. But no human effort could prevent what was about to happen.

Early on Sunday morning, while it was still dark, Mary Magdalene and other women went to the tomb with spices to properly prepare Jesus's body. They wondered who would roll away the heavy stone for them. But when they arrived, they found the stone already rolled away and the tomb empty!

Suddenly, there was a violent earthquake, and an angel whose appearance was like lightning appeared. The guards were so afraid they fell like dead men. The angel told the women, "Don't be afraid. I know you are looking for Jesus, who was crucified. He is not here; He has risen, just as He said! Come and see the place where He lay, then go quickly and tell His disciples."

The women ran from the tomb, afraid yet filled with joy. Mary Magdalene found Peter and John, who raced to the tomb. John arrived first and looked in, seeing the strips of linen lying there. Peter went inside and saw not only the linen strips, but also the burial cloth that had been around Jesus's head, folded up by itself. The disciples went home, amazed but still not fully understanding.

Mary Magdalene stayed at the tomb, crying. As she wept, she looked inside and saw two angels where Jesus's body had been. They asked her why she was crying. "They have taken my Lord away," she said, "and I don't know where they have put Him." Then she turned and saw someone she thought was the gardener. He asked her the same question, and she begged Him to tell her where Jesus's body was. Then He said one word – "Mary" – and she recognized His voice. It was Jesus!

That same day, Jesus appeared to two disciples walking to Emmaus, explaining how all the Scriptures pointed to Him. He appeared to His disciples behind locked doors, showing them His hands and side. A week later, He appeared again when Thomas was present, allowing the doubting disciple to touch His wounds. By the sea of Galilee, He cooked breakfast for His disciples and restored Peter, who had denied Him three times, by asking him three times, "Do you love me?"

For forty days, Jesus appeared to His followers, giving many convincing proofs that He was alive. He explained how His death and resurrection fulfilled God's plan for salvation. Finally, He gathered His disciples on a mountain and gave them what we call the Great Commission: "All authority in heaven and on earth has been given to me. Therefore, go and make disciples of all nations, baptizing them in the name of the Father and of the Son and of the Holy Spirit, and teaching them to obey everything I have commanded you. And surely I am with you always, to the very end of the age."

🔍 Time Travel Corner:

Welcome to ancient Jerusalem during Passover! The city would have been packed with pilgrims, with perhaps 200,000 people crowding its streets. Archaeologists have discovered the actual paths Jesus would have walked, including the ancient stone pavement where Pilate judged Him. They've found evidence of crucifixion practices, including a heel bone with a nail through it. The tomb where Jesus was laid would have been cut into solid rock, with a large disk-shaped stone that rolled in a groove to seal the entrance.

💡 Did You Know?

- The crown of thorns was probably made from a local plant with thorns up to 4 inches long

- The cross beam Jesus carried weighed about 100 pounds

- The temple curtain that tore was 60 feet high and very thick

- Roman guards would face death if they fell asleep on duty

- The stone covering Jesus's tomb probably weighed 1-2 tons

- Jesus showed himself to more than 500 people after His resurrection

🧠 Think About It:

1. Why did Jesus pray "not my will, but yours" when He knew what was coming?

2. How did different people react to Jesus's death and resurrection?

3. Why did Jesus appear to Mary Magdalene first?

4. What made the disciples willing to die for their belief in the resurrection?

5. How does Jesus's resurrection change everything for us today?

✏️ Your Turn:

- Create a timeline of events from Thursday night to Sunday morning

- Draw a map of Jerusalem showing where key events happened

- Write a diary entry as one of the women who found the empty tomb

- Design what the garden tomb might have looked like

- List all the people Jesus appeared to after His resurrection

↖ Dig Deeper:

Archaeological discoveries show:

- The probable location of Golgotha

- Ancient tombs similar to Jesus's

- The foundations of Pilate's judgment hall

- First-century Roman execution tools

- Evidence of earthquake damage from that time

👤👤👤👤 Family Talk:

- What does Jesus's sacrifice mean to our family?

- How can we show our gratitude for what Jesus did?

- What would we have done if we were there?

- How do we share the good news of Jesus's resurrection?

- What difference does the resurrection make in our daily lives?

Chapter 11:

Saul to Paul - From Persecutor to Preacher

Have you ever met someone who completely changed – someone who used to be one way but became totally different? The story of how Saul became Paul is one of the most dramatic transformations in the Bible. It shows us that no one is too far from God's reach, and that God can use our past experiences – even the bad ones – for good.

Our story begins with a young man named Saul, who thought he was doing God a favor by trying to destroy the early Christian church. He was highly educated, a Pharisee who had studied under the best teachers, and he was convinced that followers of Jesus were dangerous to the Jewish faith. He went from house to house in Jerusalem, dragging Christians to prison. He even held the coats of those who stoned Stephen, the first Christian martyr, approving of his death.

Saul was so determined to stop Christianity from spreading that he got permission from the high priest to go to Damascus, about 150 miles away, to arrest any followers of Jesus he found there and bring them back to Jerusalem in chains. He set out on horseback with a group of men, breathing out threats and murder against the Lord's disciples. But God had other plans.

As Saul neared Damascus around noon, suddenly a light from heaven, brighter than the sun, flashed around him and his companions. He fell to the ground and heard a voice saying, "Saul, Saul, why do you persecute me?"

Shaking, Saul asked, "Who are you, Lord?"

"I am Jesus, whom you are persecuting," the voice replied. "Now get up and go into the city, and you will be told what you must do."

The men traveling with Saul stood speechless. They heard the sound but didn't see anyone. When Saul got up from the ground and opened his eyes, he discovered he was blind. His companions had to lead him by the hand into Damascus, where for three days he didn't eat or drink anything. The mighty persecutor had become helpless as a child.

Meanwhile, in Damascus, there was a disciple named Ananias. The Lord appeared to him in a vision, telling him to go to the house where Saul was staying and place his hands on him to restore his sight. Ananias was terrified – everyone knew about Saul and the harm he had done to believers in Jerusalem.

"Lord," Ananias protested, "I have heard many reports about this man and all the harm he has done to your holy people in Jerusalem. And he has come here with authority from the chief priests to arrest all who call on your name."

But the Lord said, "Go! This man is my chosen instrument to carry my name before the Gentiles and their kings and before the people of Israel. I will show him how much he must suffer for my name."

So Ananias went. When he placed his hands on Saul, something like scales fell from Saul's eyes, and he could see again. He got up and was baptized, and after taking some food, he regained his strength. The persecutor of Christians had become a follower of Christ.

The change in Saul was immediate and dramatic. He began preaching in the Damascus synagogues that Jesus is the Son of God. People were astonished – wasn't this the same man who had come to arrest believers? Some were convinced by his powerful arguments that Jesus was the Messiah, but others plotted to kill him. Late one night, his followers had to lower him in a basket through an opening in the city wall so he could escape.

When Saul returned to Jerusalem, the believers there were afraid of him – they couldn't believe he was really a disciple. But Barnabas, whose name means "son of encouragement," spoke up for him. He told the apostles how Saul had seen the Lord and had preached fearlessly in Damascus. Finally, they accepted him.

Now known by his Greek name Paul, he faced opposition everywhere he went. Jews who rejected his message about Jesus tried to stone him. Some Gentiles (non-Jews) got angry when he told them to turn from their idols. He was beaten, imprisoned, and shipwrecked. But nothing could stop him from sharing the good news about Jesus.

Paul went on three major missionary journeys, traveling thousands of miles by land and sea. He established churches in major cities across the Roman Empire – places like Philippi, Thessalonica, Corinth, and Ephesus. He worked as a tentmaker to support himself, often preaching in the evening after working all day.

In each city, Paul would usually start by preaching in the Jewish synagogue. He would explain from the Scriptures how Jesus fulfilled all the prophecies about the Messiah. Some Jews believed, but others rejected his message. Then he would turn to the Gentiles, explaining that God's salvation was for everyone who believed in Jesus, not just the Jews.

One of Paul's most amazing experiences happened in Lystra. After he and Barnabas healed a lame man, the crowd thought they were Greek gods and tried to offer sacrifices to them! Paul and Barnabas tore their clothes in dismay and rushed into the crowd, shouting, "We are only human beings like you!" But the next day, some opponents arrived and turned the same crowd against them. They stoned Paul and dragged him out of the city, thinking he was dead. But he got up and went right back into the city!

Paul's deep love for Jesus and the churches he started shines through in the letters he wrote. He reminded the Philippians to rejoice always, taught the Corinthians about love, encouraged the Thessalonians about Christ's return, and explained to the Romans how we are saved by faith. These letters, which became part of the New Testament, continue to guide and encourage Christians today.

One of Paul's most dramatic adventures happened on his way to Rome. He was being taken there as a prisoner because he had appealed to Caesar after being falsely accused. During the voyage, a terrible storm struck. For two weeks, the ship was driven by the wind, and everyone thought they would die. But Paul encouraged them, saying an angel had told him that everyone would survive, though the ship would be destroyed. That's exactly what happened – the ship ran aground and broke apart, but all 276 people made it safely to shore by swimming or floating on pieces of the wreck.

In Rome, Paul was placed under house arrest but was allowed to receive visitors. For two years, he continued teaching about Jesus to everyone who came to see him. Even in chains, he saw his situation as an opportunity to share the gospel with the Roman guards who were assigned to watch him.

According to tradition, Paul was eventually released and continued his missionary work until he was arrested again during Emperor Nero's persecution of Christians. He wrote his final letter to Timothy from prison, saying, "I have fought the good fight, I have finished the race, I have kept the faith." He was executed in Rome, but his impact on Christianity had only begun.

Paul's life shows us how completely God can change someone. The man who once tried to destroy the church became its greatest missionary. He went from arresting Christians to being arrested for Christ. He suffered beatings, shipwrecks, hunger, and imprisonment, yet he called these troubles "light and momentary" compared to the joy of knowing Jesus.

Through Paul's ministry, Christianity spread from being a small Jewish movement to becoming a faith that reached across the Roman Empire. His writings explain many of the core beliefs Christians hold today, and his missionary journeys set a pattern for taking the gospel to new places. Most importantly, his life shows that no one is beyond God's reach, and that God can use our past experiences – even the painful ones – to help others.

🔍 Time Travel Corner:

Welcome to the first-century Roman Empire! Thanks to Roman roads and sea routes, people could travel throughout the Mediterranean world. Cities like Ephesus and Corinth were major trading centers with theaters, temples, and marketplaces. Ships like the one Paul was shipwrecked in were large grain carriers that could hold hundreds of passengers. Archaeologists have found remains of ancient synagogues where Paul would have preached, and inscriptions mentioning places and people from his letters.

💡 Did You Know?

- Paul traveled about 10 000 miles on his missionary journeys

- Letters in ancient times were written on papyrus scrolls

- The city of Ephesus had a theater that could seat 25,000 people

- Roman citizens like Paul had special legal rights

- Ships in Paul's time didn't have compasses – they navigated by stars

- Paul probably spoke at least three languages: Hebrew, Greek, and Aramaic

🧠 Think About It:

1. Why did God choose someone who hated Christians to become a great missionary?

2. How did Paul's education and Roman citizenship help his ministry?

3. What made Paul continue despite all his hardships?

4. Why were Paul's letters so important for the early church?

5. How can God use our past experiences to help others?

Your Turn:

- Draw a map of Paul's missionary journeys

- Write a diary entry as if you were with Paul during the shipwreck

- Create a timeline of Paul's life from persecutor to missionary

- Design a Roman ship like the one Paul traveled on

- List all the different places Paul visited

Dig Deeper:

Archaeological discoveries show:

- Remains of the ancient cities Paul visited

- Roman roads he would have traveled

- Inscriptions mentioning people from his letters

- Ancient synagogues where he preached

- Types of tools used by tentmakers

Family Talk:

- How has God changed people we know?

- What can we learn from Paul about sharing our faith?

- How do we handle opposition when doing what's right?

- What gifts has God given us to serve others?

- How can our family be missionaries where we live?

Chapter 12:

A Glimpse of Heaven - John's Vision

Have you ever wondered what heaven will be like? Or what will happen at the very end of time? God gave the apostle John an amazing vision that answers some of these questions. His vision, recorded in the book of Revelation, shows us that no matter how difficult things get, God wins in the end.

Our story begins when John was an old man, probably in his 90s. He was the last living apostle who had walked with Jesus, and he had been exiled to a small rocky island called Patmos because he wouldn't stop telling people about Jesus. But even in this lonely place, God had something special planned for him.

One Sunday, John heard a voice behind him that sounded like a trumpet. When he turned around, he saw something so amazing it made him fall down like a dead man. There stood Jesus, but not as John remembered Him from their days in Galilee. Now He appeared in glorious light, with eyes like blazing fire, hair as white as snow, and a face shining like the sun. His voice was like the sound of rushing waters, and He held seven stars in His right hand.

"Don't be afraid," Jesus told John. "I am the First and the Last. I am the Living One; I was dead, and now look, I am alive for ever and ever! Write on a scroll what you see and send it to the seven churches."

Then John saw a door standing open in heaven, and the same voice said, "Come up here, and I will show you what must take place after this." Immediately, he was caught up in the Spirit and saw something that took his breath away: a magnificent throne surrounded by a rainbow as brilliant as an emerald. On the throne sat One whose appearance was like jasper and ruby, too glorious to describe in human words.

Around the throne were twenty-four other thrones with elders dressed in white, wearing gold crowns. From the main throne came flashes of lightning and rolls of thunder. Four amazing living creatures surrounded it, covered with eyes and having different faces – one like a lion, one like an ox, one like a human, and one like a flying eagle. Day and night they never stopped saying: "Holy, holy, holy is the Lord God Almighty, who was, and is, and is to come."

John saw a scroll in the right hand of the One on the throne, sealed with seven seals A mighty angel called out, "Who is worthy to break the seals and open the scroll?" But no one in heaven or earth was found worthy. John began to weep, but one of the elders said, "Don't cry! Look, the Lion of the tribe of Judah, the Root of David, has won the right to open the scroll."

Then John saw a Lamb, looking as if it had been slain, standing at the center of the throne. This was Jesus, portrayed as both the powerful Lion and the sacrificial Lamb. When He took the scroll, millions of angels burst into song: "Worthy is the Lamb, who was slain, to receive power and wealth and wisdom and strength and honor and glory and praise!"

As the Lamb opened each seal, John saw visions of both trouble and triumph. He saw the famous four horsemen – representing conquest, war, famine, and death. But he also saw martyrs who had died for their faith being given white robes and told to rest a little longer until their full number was complete.

John saw incredible sights that were both wonderful and terrifying. He watched as angels blew seven trumpets, each bringing different events to earth. He saw a great battle in heaven where Michael and his angels fought against a dragon – Satan – and his evil angels. The dragon was hurled down to earth, but he continued to make war against God's people.

Then John saw a beast rising from the sea, representing an evil empire that would persecute believers. Another beast from the earth performed miraculous signs to deceive people. But John also saw 144,000 faithful people standing with the Lamb on Mount Zion, singing a new song that only they could learn.

One of the most beautiful visions John saw was of Jesus returning as a conquering King. Heaven opened, and there was a white horse. Its rider, called Faithful and True, wore a robe dipped in blood, and the armies of heaven followed Him on white horses. On His robe and thigh was written: "KING OF KINGS AND LORD OF LORDS."

John watched as Satan was bound for a thousand years, then released for a final battle, and finally defeated forever. Then came the most solemn scene: a great white throne appeared, and all the dead were judged according to what they had done, as recorded in the books of heaven.

But the best was yet to come. John saw a new heaven and a new earth, for the first heaven and earth had passed away. He saw the Holy City, the New Jerusalem, coming down from heaven like a bride beautifully dressed for her husband. The city was incredible – made of pure gold, with walls of jasper and twelve gates each made from a single pearl. The foundations were decorated with every kind of precious stone, and the streets were pure gold, like transparent glass.

There was no temple in the city, because God Himself and the Lamb were its temple. The city didn't need the sun or moon to shine on it, because God's glory gave it light. The River of Life flowed from the throne, clear as crystal, and the Tree of Life grew on each side, bearing twelve crops of fruit and leaves that would heal the nations.

Best of all, John heard a loud voice from the throne saying, "Look! God's dwelling place is now among the people, and he will dwell with them. They will be his people, and God himself will be with them and be their God. He will wipe every tear from their eyes. There will be no more death or mourning or crying or pain, for the old order of things has passed away."

The angel showing John these things told him, "These words are trustworthy and true." Then Jesus Himself spoke: "Look, I am coming soon! My reward is with me, and I will give to each person according to what they have done. I am the Alpha and the Omega, the First and the Last, the Beginning and the End."

John learned that everyone who is thirsty is invited to come and drink freely from the Water of Life. The Spirit and the bride say, "Come!" And let everyone who hears say, "Come!" Whoever is thirsty should come; whoever wishes may drink freely from the Water of Life.

The book ends with Jesus saying three times, "I am coming soon!" John responded with words that Christians have echoed ever since: "Amen. Come, Lord Jesus!"

When John returned from his vision, he carefully wrote down everything he had seen, just as Jesus commanded. His message brought hope to persecuted Christians of his time, showing them that despite their suffering, God would ultimately triumph. The same message continues to encourage believers today who face difficulties – reminding us that no matter how dark things seem, Jesus wins in the end, and those who trust in Him will live with Him forever in that beautiful new city.

Many of the things John saw were mysterious, described in symbolic language that people still discuss and debate today. But the main message is clear: God is in control, Jesus will return, evil will be defeated, and God's people will live with Him forever in a perfect new world where there is no more pain, death, or tears.

🔍 Time Travel Corner:

Welcome to the island of Patmos in the late first century! This small rocky island in the Aegean Sea was a Roman prison colony. Archaeological remains show it was sparsely populated, with rocky terrain and few trees. The cave where tradition says John received his vision can still be visited today. The seven churches John wrote to were all located in what is now western Turkey, and archaeologists have uncovered remains of all these ancient cities.

💡 Did You Know?

- Patmos is only about 7 miles long and 4 miles wide

- The number 7 appears 54 times in Revelation

- The New Jerusalem would be about 1,400 miles in each direction

- The book contains over 500 references to Old Testament passages

- Roman Emperor Domitian required people to worship him as a god

- The early Christians used symbols like the lamb to secretly identify themselves

🧠 Think About It:

1. Why did God give this vision to John when he was old and in exile?

2. What does the mix of symbols (lamb, lion, bride) tell us about Jesus?

3. Why is the New Jerusalem described in such detail?

4. How does knowing the end of the story help us face difficulties today?

5. What makes heaven sound most exciting to you?

✏️ Your Turn:

- Draw what you think the New Jerusalem might look like

- Create a map showing the locations of the seven churches

- Design one of the amazing creatures John described

- Write a description of what a day in the New Earth might be like

- List all the precious stones mentioned in the New Jerusalem

Dig Deeper:

Archaeological discoveries show:

- Remains of the seven churches John wrote to

- Roman persecution records from this time

- Ancient manuscripts of Revelation

- The cave where tradition says John received his vision

- Trade routes that connected the seven churches

Family Talk:

- What are we most looking forward to about heaven?

- How can we stay faithful when following God is hard?

- What helps us remember that God wins in the end?

- How can we share this hope with others?

- What would we like to ask John about his vision?

Chapter 13:

Ruth – A Story of Loyalty and Love

In the midst of loss and hardship, one choice can change everything. That's what happened in the story of Ruth, a young woman from the land of Moab who chose to follow her mother-in-law into an uncertain future. Her tale isn't just about family loyalty – it's about how faith, love, and determination can turn the darkest times into something beautiful.

Our story begins during a time of famine in Israel, when food was scarce and times were hard. A man named Elimelech, his wife Naomi, and their two sons left their home in Bethlehem to find food in the country of Moab. This wasn't an easy decision – Moab was often an enemy of Israel, and its people worshipped different gods. But they felt they had no choice if they wanted to survive.

In Moab, their sons married two local women: Orpah and Ruth. For about ten years, they made a life there. But then tragedy struck. First Elimelech died, leaving Naomi a widow in a foreign land. Then both of her sons died too. Naomi was left alone with her two daughters-in-law, far from her homeland, with no one to provide for them in a culture where women depended on male relatives for survival.

When Naomi heard that the famine in Israel was over, she decided to return home to Bethlehem. But first, she told Orpah and Ruth to go back to their own families. "Go back, each of you, to your mother's home," she said. "May the Lord show you kindness, as you have shown kindness to your dead husbands and to me."

The three women stood on the road weeping. At first, both daughters-in-law insisted on going with Naomi. But she urged them to think carefully about their decision: "Return home, my daughters. Why would you come with me? Am I going to have any more sons, who could become your husbands? I am too old to have another husband. Even if I thought there was still hope for me—even if I had a husband tonight and then gave birth to sons—would you wait until they grew up?"

Orpah finally kissed Naomi goodbye and returned to her family – a sensible choice in those times. But Ruth clung to Naomi and spoke words so beautiful they're still quoted today: "Don't urge me to leave you or to turn back from you. Where you go I will go, and where you stay I will stay. Your people will be my people and your God my God. Where you die I will die, and there I will be buried. May the Lord deal with me, be it ever so severely, if even death separates you and me."

When Naomi saw that Ruth was determined to go with her, she stopped urging her. Together, they made the long journey to Bethlehem. It must have been a difficult trip for both of them – Naomi returning home empty after leaving full, and Ruth leaving everything she knew to go to a foreign land where Moabites weren't always welcome.

They arrived in Bethlehem just as the barley harvest was beginning. The whole town was stirred because of them, and the women exclaimed, "Can this be Naomi?" But she told them, "Don't call me Naomi (which means 'pleasant'). Call me Mara (which means 'bitter'), because the Almighty has made my life very bitter. I went away full, but the Lord has brought me back empty."

Ruth, wanting to provide for both of them, asked Naomi's permission to go into the fields and pick up the leftover grain behind anyone in whose eyes she found favor. This was a provision in Jewish law called "gleaning" – farmers were supposed to leave some grain in their fields for the poor to collect

By God's providence, Ruth found herself gleaning in a field belonging to Boaz, a wealthy and respected man who was a relative of Naomi's late husband. When Boaz arrived from Bethlehem to check on his harvesters, he noticed Ruth and asked his foreman about her. "She is the Moabite who came back from Moab with Naomi," the foreman replied. "She asked if she could pick up the leftover grain, and she has worked hard from morning until now, except for a short rest."

Boaz went to Ruth and said, "Listen, my daughter. Don't go and glean in another field. Stay here with my servant girls. Watch where they harvest and follow them. I have told the men not to lay a hand on you. And whenever you are thirsty, go and get a drink from the water jars the men have filled."

Ruth bowed down with her face to the ground. "Why have I found such favor in your eyes," she asked, "that you notice me—a foreigner?" Boaz replied, "I've heard all about what you have done for your mother-in-law since the death of your husband—how you left your father and mother and your homeland and came to live with a people you didn't know before. May the Lord repay you for what you have done. May you be richly rewarded by the Lord, the God of Israel, under whose wings you have come to take refuge."

Boaz went even further in his kindness. He told his workers to purposely pull out some stalks from their bundles and leave them for Ruth to find. He invited her to eat with his harvesters and even served her himself. That evening, when Ruth brought home all the grain she had gathered—about thirty pounds of barley—Naomi asked where she had gleaned. When she heard it was in Boaz's field, Naomi exclaimed, "The Lord bless him! He has not stopped showing his kindness to the living and the dead. That man is our close relative; he is one of our guardian-redeemers."

When the harvest season was ending, Naomi came up with a bold plan. She explained to Ruth that Boaz, as a close relative, could be their "kinsman-redeemer" – someone who had the right and responsibility to help relatives in serious need. She told Ruth to wash, put on perfume, and dress in her best clothes, then go to the threshing floor where Boaz would be spending the night guarding his harvest.

"Wait until he has finished eating and drinking," Naomi instructed. "When he lies down, note the place where he is lying. Then go and uncover his feet and lie down. He will tell you what to do." This might sound strange to us today, but it was actually Ruth's way of asking Boaz to fulfill his role as kinsman-redeemer by marrying her.

Ruth did exactly as Naomi said. In the middle of the night, Boaz woke up startled to find someone lying at his feet. "Who are you?" he asked. "I am your servant Ruth," she replied. "Spread the corner of your garment over me, since you are a guardian-redeemer of our family." This was a culturally appropriate way of asking for marriage and protection.

Boaz was deeply moved by Ruth's request. "The Lord bless you, my daughter," he said. "This kindness is greater than what you showed earlier: You have not run after the younger men, whether rich or poor. And now, don't be afraid. I will do for you al you ask. All the people of my town know that you are a woman of noble character."

But there was a complication. There was another relative who was closer than Boaz and had the first right to be the kinsman-redeemer. Boaz promised to settle the matter the very next day. He sent Ruth home before dawn with six measures of barley, so she wouldn't return to Naomi empty-handed.

The next morning, Boaz went to the town gate, where legal matters were settled. When the closer relative came by, Boaz gathered ten elders as witnesses and presented the situation. The man was interested in redeeming Elimelech's property until he learned he would also need to marry Ruth. Concerned about complicating his own inheritance, he removed his sandal (a legal gesture showing he was giving up his right) and told Boaz to be the redeemer.

With the legal matters settled, Boaz announced to all the witnesses, "Today you are witnesses that I have bought from Naomi all the property of Elimelech, Kilion, and Mahlon. I have also acquired Ruth the Moabite, Mahlon's widow, as my wife, in order to maintain the name of the dead with his property, so that his name will not disappear from among his family or from his hometown."

Boaz and Ruth were married, and God blessed them with a son. The women of Bethlehem celebrated with Naomi, saying, "Praise be to the Lord, who this day has not left you without a guardian-redeemer. May he become famous throughout Israel! He will renew your life and sustain you in your old age. For your daughter-in-law, who loves you and who is better to you than seven sons, has given him birth."

Naomi took the child and cared for him as her own. The women of the neighborhood gave him the name Obed, which means "servant." This baby would grow up to become the grandfather of King David, and through this family line, many generations later, Jesus Christ would be born.

The story of Ruth shows how God can bring hope out of hopelessness and joy out of sorrow. Ruth's decision to stay with Naomi led her to become part of God's bigger plan, though she couldn't have known it at the time. Her story reminds us that kindness, loyalty, and doing what's right even in hard times can lead to blessings we never expected.

The book of Ruth also shows us how God cares for all people, regardless of their background. Ruth was a foreigner from Moab, but she became one of only a few women mentioned in Jesus's family tree. Her story teaches us that when we choose to trust God and show faithful love to others, He can use our lives in amazing ways.

🔍 Time Travel Corner:

Welcome to ancient Bethlehem during the time of the judges! Archaeological discoveries show how people lived during this period. Farmers used sharp stones attached to wooden boards to harvest grain. The threshing floor was a flat, hard surface where grain was separated from chaff, often located on c hilltop to catch the wind. Houses were typically small, with one main room and a roof where people could sleep in warm weather. The town gate, where Boaz settled legal matters, was the center of community life.

💡 Did You Know?

- The barley harvest usually took place in April–May

- Gleaning was an ancient form of welfare system

- A kinsman-redeemer had to be a close male relative

- The sandal ceremony was a legal contract symbol

- Moab was about 50 miles from Bethlehem

- The events probably took place around 1100 BC

💭 Think About It:

1. Why did Ruth choose to stay with Naomi when she could have gone home?

2. How did Boaz show kindness beyond what the law required?

3. What made Ruth stand out as "a woman of noble character"?

4. How did God work through ordinary events to accomplish His plan?

5. What can we learn about loyalty and faithfulness from this story?

✏️ Your Turn:

- Draw a map of Ruth's journey from Moab to Bethlehem

- Create a timeline showing the key events in Ruth's story

- Write a diary entry as Ruth on her first day gleaning

- Design what the threshing floor might have looked like

- List all the ways Boaz showed kindness to Ruth

⛏ Dig Deeper:

Archaeological discoveries show:

- Ancient farming tools from this period

- Remains of city gates where business was conducted

- Grain storage systems

- Types of houses people lived in

- Evidence of trade between Israel and Moab

👥👥👥👥 Family Talk:

- How can we show loyalty to family and friends?

- When have we seen God turn hard times into blessings?

- How can we welcome people who are different from us?

- What does Ruth's story teach us about God's care?

- How can we trust God when our future seems uncertain?

Chapter 14:

Solomon - The Wisest King

Have you ever wished you could have anything you wanted? Imagine if God appeared to you in a dream and said, "Ask for whatever you want me to give you." That's exactly what happened to young King Solomon. His choice – and what happened because of it – teaches us one of the most important lessons in the Bible.

Solomon was the son of King David and Bathsheba. When David was old, he chose Solomon to be the next king of Israel, even though Solomon wasn't his oldest son. "Be strong and show yourself a man," David told Solomon before he died. "Walk in God's ways and keep his commands, and you will succeed in all you do."

Soon after becoming king, Solomon went to Gibeon to offer sacrifices to God. That right, God appeared to him in a dream with an amazing offer: "Ask for whatever you want me to give you." Solomon could have asked for anything – riches, long life, victory over his enemies. But instead, he showed remarkable humility.

"Lord my God," Solomon replied, "you have made your servant king in place of my father David. But I am only a little child and do not know how to carry out my duties.

Your servant is here among the people you have chosen, a great people, too numerous to count. So give your servant a discerning heart to govern your people and to distinguish between right and wrong."

God was so pleased with Solomon's request that He gave him more than he asked for. "Since you have asked for wisdom to govern justly, and not for long life, wealth, or the death of your enemies, I will give you a wise and discerning heart. In fact, there will never be anyone as wise as you. But I will also give you what you didn't ask for – both riches and honor. And if you walk in my ways as your father David did, I will give you a long life too."

Soon after this, Solomon faced a challenging test that would demonstrate his wisdom to all Israel. Two women came before him with a terrible dispute. They lived in the same house, and each had given birth to a baby boy within days of each other. During the night, one of the babies died when his mother accidentally rolled over on him. This mother switched the babies, putting her dead son next to the other woman and taking the living baby for herself.

In the morning, the second woman woke to find a dead baby beside her, but when she looked closely, she knew it wasn't her son. Both women came before Solomon, each claiming the living child was hers.

How could Solomon determine which woman was telling the truth? There were no witnesses, no evidence, and both women seemed completely convinced they were right. Solomon's solution shocked everyone. "Bring me a sword," he commanded. When they brought it, he said, "Cut the living child in two and give half to one woman and half to the other."

The first woman didn't hesitate: "Please, my lord, give her the living baby! Don't kill him!"

But the second woman said, "Neither I nor you shall have him. Cut him in two!"

Then Solomon gave his verdict: "Give the living baby to the first woman. Do not kill him; she is his mother." The true mother's love for her child was revealed by her willingness to give him up rather than see him harmed. When people heard about this judgment, they were in awe of Solomon's wisdom.

This was just the beginning of Solomon's remarkable reign. His wisdom surpassed that of all the other kings, and he became famous throughout the surrounding nations. He composed three thousand proverbs and wrote one thousand and five songs. He could speak with authority about plants, animals, birds, reptiles, and fish. Kings and queens traveled from far away to test his wisdom with hard questions.

The most famous of these visitors was the Queen of Sheba. She arrived with a great caravan of camels carrying spices, gold, and precious stones. She came to test Solomon with difficult questions, but he answered them all. When she saw his wisdom, his palace, the food on his table, the seating of his officials, and the attending servants in their robes, she was overwhelmed.

"The report I heard in my own country about your achievements and wisdom was true," she told Solomon. "But I didn't believe it until I came and saw with my own eyes. In fact, not even half was told to me; your wisdom and prosperity far exceed the report I heard!"

Under Solomon's reign, Israel reached its greatest height of power and prosperity. He built a magnificent temple for God in Jerusalem, using the finest materials and craftsmen. The temple took seven years to build and was covered in gold, with intricate carvings of cherubim, palm trees, and flowers. When it was completed, the glory of the Lord filled it in the form of a cloud, just as had happened with the tabernacle in Moses' time.

Solomon also built a grand palace for himself, which took thirteen years to complete. He developed trading partnerships with other nations, and his ships brought back gold, silver, ivory, and exotic animals. Silver became as common as stones in Jerusalem, and cedar as plentiful as sycamore-fig trees.

But with all his wisdom, Solomon eventually made some serious mistakes. God had commanded Israel's kings not to multiply horses, wives, or gold for themselves, yet Solomon did all three. He had 1,400 chariots and 12,000 horses. His wealth became legendary. Most seriously, he had 700 wives of royal birth and 300 concubines, many from nations that worshiped other gods.

As Solomon grew older, his foreign wives turned his heart away from fully following the Lord. He built high places for their gods - including Chemosh, the detestable god of Moab, and Molech, the horrible god of the Ammonites. This was especielly tragic because God had appeared to Solomon twice and specifically warned him about turning to other gods.

The Lord became angry w th Solomon and told him, "Since this is your attitude and you have not kept my covenant and my decrees, which I commanded you, I will most certainly tear the kingdom away from you and give it to one of your subordinctes. Nevertheless, for the sake of David your father, I will not do it during your lifetime. I will tear it out of the hand of your son."

Despite these mistakes, Solomon's wisdom continues to benefit us today through the books he wrote: Proverbs, Ecclesiastes, and the Song of Songs. In Proverbs, he shares practical wisdom for daily living. In Ecclesiastes, he reflects on his search for meaning in life, concluding that everything apart from God is meaningless. His final advice? "Fear God and keep his commandments, for this is the duty of all mankind."

Solomon's life teaches us that wisdom itself isn't enough - we must continue to follow God with all our heart. He had more wisdom than anyone who ever lived, but knowledge without obedience eventually led to foolish choices. Yet God's mercy remained - though the kingdom would be divided, God kept His promise to David by maintaining a remnant of his descendants on the throne.

Solomon ruled Israel for forty years. When he died, the kingdom was at its peak of prosperity but on the verge of division. His son Rehoboam would soon face a critical test that would split the kingdom in two, just as God had warned.

I'll add our six standard supplementary sections:

🔍 Time Travel Corner:

Welcome to Jerusalem during Solomon's reign, around 950 BC! Archaeologists have uncovered evidence of the massive building projects from this period. The temple was built on a huge platform that still exists today. Solomon's palace complex covered about 10 acres. Trade routes stretched from Egypt to Mesopotamia, bringing exotic goods through Jerusalem. The city was protected by massive walls and gates, some of which have been discovered by archaeologists. The remains of Solomon's stables and chariot cities show the scale of his military power.

💡 Did You Know?

- Solomon's temple took 7 years to build but his palace took 13 years

- The temple used so much gold that its weight wasn't recorded

- Solomon received 25 tons of gold yearly in tribute

- His drinking cups were all made of gold

- The temple platform required stones weighing up to 500 tons

- Ships had to sail for three years to bring back exotic goods

🧠 Think About It:

1. Why did Solomon ask for wisdom instead of riches or power?

2. How did Solomon's early humility compare to his later pride?

3. Why did God give Solomon more than he asked for?

4. What made Solomon's foreign marriages so dangerous spiritually?

5. How can someone so wise make such unwise choices?

📣 Your Turn:

- Draw what you think Solomon's temple looked like

- Design a trade route map showing Solomon's commercial networks

- Create a timeline of Solomon's major building projects

- Write your own proverb about wisdom

- List all the different kinds of things Solomon studied

⛏ Dig Deeper:

Archaeological discoveries show:

- Remains of Solomon's gates in various cities

- Evidence of extensive trade networks

- Ancient copper mines from Solomon's time

- Building techniques used in the temple period

- Pottery showing cultural connections with other nations

👥👥👥👥 Family Talk:

- What would we ask for if God gave us one request?

- How can we use wisdom to help others?

- What can we learn from Solomon's mistakes?

- How do we keep our hearts focused on God when blessed?

- What's the difference between knowledge and wisdom?

Chapter 15:

John the Baptist - Preparing the Way

Have you ever had to wait for something really important? Maybe you've counted down the days until your birthday, or waited eagerly for a special event. The people of Israel had been waiting for hundreds of years – waiting for the Messiah that God had promised to send. Before Jesus began His public ministry, God sent someone special to help people get ready: John the Baptist.

John wasn't your typical religious teacher. He lived in the wilderness, wore clothes made of camel's hair with a leather belt, and ate locusts and wild honey. He might have seemed strange to people, but he was exactly who God had promised to send. Hundreds of years earlier, the prophet Isaiah had written about a "voice calling in the wilderness: 'Prepare the way for the Lord, make straight paths for him.'" That voice was John.

People came from all over Judea and Jerusalem to hear John preach by the Jordan River. His message was powerful but simple: "Repent, for the kingdom of heaven is near!" He told people to turn away from their sins and be baptized as a sign that they wanted to change. He wasn't afraid to challenge anyone – from common people to religious leaders to King Herod himself.

When people came to be baptized, John didn't just dunk them in the water and send them home. He called for real change in their lives. When tax collectors asked what they should do, he told them to collect only what was required and not cheat people. When soldiers asked, he told them not to extort money or accuse people falsely. He told everyone who had extra food or clothing to share with those who had none.

But he was especially tough on the religious leaders – the Pharisees and Sadducees – who came to watch. "You brood of vipers!" he called them. "Who warned you to flee from the coming wrath? Produce fruit in keeping with repentance. Don't just say to yourselves, 'We have Abraham as our father.' God can raise up children for Abraham from these stones!"

John's straight talk and powerful message drew such large crowds that people began to wonder if he might be the Messiah himself. But John quickly set them straight: "I baptize you with water for repentance. But after me comes one who is more powerful than I, whose sandals I am not worthy to carry. He will baptize you with the Holy Spirit and fire."

One day, while John was baptizing people in the Jordan River, Jesus himself came to be baptized. John was shocked. "I need to be baptized by you," he protested, "and do you come to me?" But Jesus insisted: "Let it be so now; it is proper for us to do this to fulfill all righteousness."

As Jesus came up out of the water, something amazing happened. The heavens opened, and John saw the Spirit of God descending like a dove and landing on Jesus. Then a voice from heaven said, "This is my Son, whom I love; with him I am well pleased."

The next day, when John saw Jesus walking by, he told his disciples, "Look, the Lamb of God, who takes away the sin of the world! This is the one I meant when I said, 'A man who comes after me has surpassed me because he was before me.'" Some of John's own disciples left him to follow Jesus, which was exactly what John wanted. "He must become greater," John said, "I must become less."

But John's ministry wasn't over. He continued preaching and baptizing, always pointing people toward Jesus. However, his bold preaching soon got him into trouble with King Herod Antipas. John had publicly criticized Herod for marrying his brother's wife, Herodias. This was more than just palace gossip – John was calling out sin and corruption at the highest levels of power.

Herod arrested John and put him in prison. Even there, John continued his ministry, sending his disciples to ask Jesus, "Are you the one who is to come, or should we expect someone else?" Jesus sent back word about all the miracles and teachings that fulfilled the prophecies about the Messiah, encouraging John that his work had not been in vain.

But Herodias held a grudge against John and looked for a way to have him killed. Her chance came during Herod's birthday celebration. Herodias's daughter danced for the guests, and Herod was so pleased that he promised her anything she wanted - up to half his kingdom. Prompted by her mother, she asked for John's head on a platter.

Though Herod was troubled by this request – he actually feared John and knew he was a righteous man – he had made his promise in front of all his guests. So he ordered John to be beheaded in prison. When Jesus heard about John's death, he withdrew by boat to a solitary place, showing his deep respect and care for his cousin who had prepared the way for him.

John's death might have seemed like a tragedy – a powerful voice for God silenced by a corrupt king's rash promise. But his impact went far beyond his lifetime. He had fulfilled exactly the role God had planned for him: preparing people's hearts for Jesus and pointing them toward the Messiah.

Jesus himself gave John the highest praise, saying, "Truly I tell you, among those born of women there has not risen anyone greater than John the Baptist." He called John a "burning and shining lamp" and said he was the "Elijah" that the prophets had said would come before the Messiah.

John's style of ministry was unique. Unlike the religious leaders who stayed in the cities and synagogues, he preached in the wilderness, calling people to come out and hear God's message. His simple lifestyle – wearing camel's hair and eating locusts and wild honey – showed that he practiced what he preached about not being attached to worldly comforts.

His message still challenges us today. Like the people of his time, we need to examine our lives and "produce fruit in keeping with repentance." Just as he told soldiers and tax collectors to be honest and fair, and told people with extra to share with those in need, his practical message of living righteously applies to our daily lives.

Most importantly, John showed us what it means to be truly humble. Even when he had a huge following, he never tried to make himself more important than he was. His whole mission was to point people to Jesus, and he was happy to step aside when Jesus began His ministry. "He must become greater; I must become less" became the theme of his life.

John was the last and greatest of the Old Testament prophets, standing at the turning point between the old covenant and the new. He was the bridge between the prophecies about the Messiah and their fulfillment in Jesus. Like a herald announcing a king's arrival, John prepared the way for Jesus to begin His ministry of salvation.

🔍 Time Travel Corner:

Welcome to the Jordan River Valley in the first century! Archaeological findings show this area was sparsely populated but had several places suitable for baptism. The traditional site of Jesus's baptism, called "Bethany Beyond the Jordan," has steps cut into the riverbank from that time period. The wilderness where John lived was rugged terrain with caves where people could shelter. Locusts were a common food source for poor people, and wild honey could be found in rock crevices and tree hollows.

💡 *Did You Know?*

- Camel hair clothing was durable but rough and uncomfortable

- The Jordan River was much wider and deeper in John's time

- Locusts are still eaten in parts of the Middle East today

- John and Jesus were cousins through their mothers

- The journey from Jerusalem to the Jordan River took about a day

- Herod's fortress where John was imprisoned can still be visited

🗨 Think About It:

1. Why did God choose someone so unusual to prepare the way for Jesus?

2. What made John's message so powerful that people traveled far to hear him?

3. Why was John willing to risk his life to speak truth to power?

4. How did John show true humility while having such a large following?

5. What can we learn from John about pointing others to Jesus?

✏ Your Turn:

- Draw a map showing where John baptized along the Jordan River

- Create a timeline of John's life from birth to death

- Write a diary entry as someone who went to hear John preach

- Design what John's wilderness camp might have looked like

- List all the prophecies John fulfilled

⬈ Dig Deeper:

Archaeological discoveries show:

- Ancient baptismal sites along the Jordan

- Remains of Herod's fortress where John was imprisoned

- Evidence of wilderness settlements from this period

- First-century ritual bathing pools

- Pottery and coins from John's time

👥👥👥👤 Family Talk:

- How can we prepare our hearts to follow Jesus?

- What does it mean to "make straight paths" for God in our lives?

- How can we be bold in standing up for what's right?

- What does true humility look like in our daily lives?

- How can we point others to Jesus like John did?

Chapter 16:

Jonah – Running from God

Have you ever tried to run away from something you knew you should do? Maybe it was a chore you didn't want to complete, or a difficult conversation you needed to have. If so, you'll understand how Jonah felt when God gave him a job he didn't want to do. His story shows us that we can't run from God – and more importantly, that God's mercy is bigger than we can imagine.

Our story begins when God spoke to Jonah: "Go to the great city of Nineveh and preach against it, because its wickedness has come up before me." This was no easy assignment. Nineveh was the capital of Assyria, one of Israel's worst enemies. The Assyrians were known for their cruelty, and Jonah probably feared for his life at the thought of going there. But even more than that, Jonah didn't want God to show mercy to his enemies!

So Jonah did something that seems almost funny when you think about it – he tried to run away from God. He went down to Joppa, found a ship heading for Tarshish (in the opposite direction from Nineveh), and set sail. He probably thought that if he left the land of Israel, he would be leaving God's presence. But Jonah was about to learn that you can't hide from the God who made the seas and the dry land.

God sent a powerful storm that threatened to break the ship apart. The sailors were terrified and began throwing cargo overboard to lighten the ship. Each man cried out to his own god for help. Meanwhile, Jonah was sound asleep in the bottom of the ship! The captain found him and said, "How can you sleep? Get up and call on your god! Maybe he will take notice of us so that we will not perish."

The sailors cast lots to find out who was responsible for this disaster, and the lot fell on Jonah. They asked him, "Tell us, who is responsible for making all this trouble for us? What kind of work do you do? Where do you come from?"

Jonah replied, "I am a Hebrew, and I worship the Lord, the God of heaven, who made the sea and the dry land." Then he told them he was running away from God. The sailors were terrified when they heard this. "What have you done?" they asked. The storm was getting worse, and they wanted to know what to do with him.

"Pick me up and throw me into the sea," Jonah said, "and it will become calm. I know that it is my fault that this great storm has come upon you." The sailors didn't want to do this. First, they tried rowing harder to return to land, but they couldn't because the storm was too fierce. Finally, they prayed to Jonah's God, asking not to be held guilty for throwing him overboard, and tossed him into the raging sea.

Immediately, the sea became calm. The sailors were so impressed by God's power that they offered sacrifices to Him and made vows. But what about Jonah? God hadn't finished with him yet. He provided a huge fish to swallow Jonah, and our reluctant prophet found himself alive inside its belly.

For three days and three nights, Jonah was inside the fish. Imagine being there – surrounded by darkness, with only the sounds of the sea and the fish's enormous heart beating. In this strange place, Jonah finally started talking to God. He prayed one of the most remarkable prayers in the Bible, saying, "In my distress I called to the Lord, and he answered me. From deep in the realm of the dead I called for help, and you listened to my cry."

Jonah acknowledged that God had every right to throw him away from His presence, but he still looked to God's holy temple. He remembered how the waters had swirled around him, seaweed wrapped around his head, and he had sunk to the roots of the mountains. But even there, God had brought his life up from the pit. Jonah ended his prayer saying, "Salvation comes from the Lord."

After three days, God commanded the fish to vomit Jonah onto dry land. Then God spoke to Jonah a second time: "Go to the great city of Nineveh and proclaim to it the message I give you." This time, Jonah obeyed.

Nineveh was an enormous city – so big it took three days to walk through it. As Jonah entered the city, he proclaimed, "Forty more days and Nineveh will be overthrown!" Something amazing happened: the Ninevites believed God! They declared a fast, and everyone, from the greatest to the least, put on sackcloth as a sign of repentance. Even the king got down from his throne, covered himself with sackcloth, and sat in the dust. He ordered everyone to call urgently on God and give up their evil ways and violence.

When God saw what they did and how they turned from their evil ways, He had compassion and did not bring on them the destruction He had threatened. But this made Jonah angry! He prayed to God, "Isn't this what I said would happen when I was still at home? That's why I tried to flee to Tarshish. I knew that you are a gracious and compassionate God, slow to anger and abounding in love, a God who relents from sending calamity."

Jonah was so upset that he asked God to let him die. He went outside the city, made himself a shelter, and sat down to see what would happen. Then God provided an object lesson. He made a leafy plant grow up quickly over Jonah, providing shade and making him very happy. But the next morning, God sent a worm to chew the plant so it withered. When the sun rose, God sent a scorching east wind, and the sun blazed on Jonah's head until he grew faint.

Again Jonah wanted to die, saying "It would be better

for me to die than to live." He was angry about the plant's death.

Then God said to Jonah, "You have been concerned about this plant, though you did not tend it or make it grow. It sprang up overnight and died overnight. And should I not have concern for Nineveh, that great city, in which there are more than a hundred and twenty thousand people who cannot tell their right hand from their left—and also many animals?"

With this question, the book of Jonah ends, leaving us to think about God's incredible mercy. Jonah had cared more about a plant that gave him shade than about thousands of people. He had received God's mercy himself inside the fish but didn't want others to receive that same mercy.

The story of Jonah teaches us many things: that we can't run from God, that God's mercy extends to everyone (even our enemies), and that God is patient with us as we learn these lessons. Jesus later referred to Jonah's three days in the fish as a sign pointing to His own death and resurrection. Like Jonah, Jesus would spend three days in darkness before bringing God's message of salvation – not just to one city, but to the whole world.

🔍 Time Travel Corner:

Welcome to ancient Nineveh, around 760 BC! Archaeologists have uncovered this massive city, located near modern-day Mosul in Iraq. The city walls were so wide that three chariots could ride side by side on top. The ruins show elaborate palaces, temples, and libraries filled with clay tablets. The Mediterranean Sea, where Jonah tried to sail away, was a busy trading route with ships carrying cargo between major ports. Ancient documents describe the types of large fish found in these waters.

💡 Did You Know?

- Nineveh's walls were 100 feet high and 50 feet thick

- The journey from Joppa to Tarshish would have taken several months

- Several species of whales and large fish lived in the Mediterranean

- Sackcloth was made from rough goat hair

- Ancient sailors often carried small idols of their gods

- The population of Nineveh was around 120,000 people

🌳 Think About It:

1. Why did Jonah think he could run away from God?

2. What made the sailors change from worshiping their gods to worshiping God?

3. How did God show mercy to both Jonah and the Ninevites?

4. Why was Jonah angry about God sparing Nineveh?

5. What does this story teach us about God's love for all people?

Your Turn:

- Draw a map showing Jonah's attempted journey to Tarshish

- Create a comic strip of the story's main events

- Write a diary entry as Jonah inside the fish

- Design what Nineveh might have looked like

- List all the miracles God performed in this story

Dig Deeper:

Archaeological discoveries show:

- Remains of Nineveh's massive walls and gates

- Ancient ships similar to the one Jonah sailed on

- Evidence of Nineveh's repentance period

- Trade routes between Joppa and Tarshish

- Clay tablets describing life in Nineveh

👤👥👤👤 Family Talk:

- When have we tried to run from something God wanted us to do?

- How can we show God's love to people we don't like?

- What makes it hard tc forgive our enemies?

- How has God shown mercy to our family?

- What can we learn frcm Jonah's mistakes?

Conclusion:

The Greatest Story Ever Told

Throughout this book, we've traveled through time and met some amazing people. We walked with Abraham as he followed God's call, stood with David as he faced Goliath, sailed with Paul as he spread the good news, and witnessed Jesus performing miracles. Each story is different, but together they tell one big story – God's story of love for people just like you and me.

We've seen how God uses all kinds of people:

- Young people like David and Mary, showing that age doesn't matter to God

- Unlikely heroes like Ruth and Esther, who changed history through their courage

- Ordinary people like Peter and John, who became extraordinary through faith

- Even people who made mistakes, like Jonah and Solomon, teaching us that God can work through imperfect people

These weren't just stories from long ago – they have important messages for us today. They show us that:

- God keeps His promises, even when we have to wait

- He can use anyone who is willing to follow Him, no matter their background

- He has a plan, even when things look difficult or impossible

- His love and mercy are bigger than we can imagine

- He is still working in our lives today, just as He worked in biblical times

In these pages, we've seen:

- Creation bloom from nothing at God's word

- A flood that covered the earth, and a rainbow of promise

- Slavery turned to freedom as the Red Sea parted

- Giants fall before shepherd boys

- Lions' mouths shut before faithful servants

- The sick healed and the dead raised

- The greatest gift of all: God's own Son coming to earth

But perhaps the most amazing thing is that you're part of this story too! God is still writing His story in the world today, and He invites each of us to be part of it. Just like Abraham stepped out in faith, like Moses led with courage, like Esther stood up for what was right, like Paul shared the good news – we too can play our part in God's continuing story.

These stories teach us that:

- God doesn't look for perfect people, just willing hearts

- The smallest acts of faithfulness can have huge impacts

- God's power is just as real today as it was then

- His love reaches to all people, everywhere

- He can turn any situation around for good

Remember, these stories aren't just history – they're "His story," and it's still being written today. As you close this book and go forward in your own life, think about how God might want to use you in His continuing story of love, redemption, and hope for the world.

Who knows? Maybe someday, someone will tell the story of how God worked through your life to help others and make the world a better place. After all, every great story in this book started with someone just like you saying "yes" to God.

The story continues... and you're part of it!

www.ingramcontent.com/pod-product-compliance
Lightning Source LLC
Chambersburg PA
CBHW071150120626
46546CB00006B/2200